Reviews

"What we call 'leadership' has not changed. What *has* changed, how-ever, are the circumstances in which we lead and the velocity of those changes. In *Leadership Unchained*, Sara Canaday provides clarity for leaders struggling to cope with challenges they face in pulling people together for a common cause. With a blend of research and practical advice, *Leadership Unchained* is a book that leaders will want on their bookshelves now…and in the future."

–John Baldoni | Internationally Recognized Executive Coach and Educator; Author of *GRACE: A Leader's Guide to a Better Us*

"In *Leadership Unchained*, Sara Canaday shares groundbreaking insights that redefine the rules for leadership as we know it. A 'must read' for anyone who values modern leadership solutions for real-world challenges. There's nothing else quite like it."

–Mark Schindele | Senior Vice President, Target

"*Leadership Unchained* offers a counterintuitive and valuable approach for current leaders and those who one day will be. The world of business has changed, and the conventional wisdom isn't working. Sara perceptively and incisively identifies the conventional leadership strengths that can become an Achilles' heel, and she pro-vides clear, actionable strategies with discerning guidance on when and how to employ them."

–Whitney Johnson | LinkedIn Influencer and Top Voices 2018; Author of *Build an A Team*

"The message that I just love from this book is to not let the skills and perspectives that were pivotal for your past success become a liability for your future productivity. In *Leadership Unchained*, Sara Canaday gives you the playbook you need for making this critical message a reality. A highly recommended read!"

> **–Andy Molinsky** | Professor of Organizational Behavior and International Management, Brandeis University; Author of *Reach: A New Strategy to Help You Step Outside Your Comfort Zone, Rise to the Challenge, and Build Confidence*

"Sara Canaday offers a unique and differing perspective on leadership in a world that is increasingly chaotic and all too demanding of every individual's time and energy. In *Leadership Unchained*, Sara looks at turning conventional leadership wisdom on its head, with insights and strategies leaders can put to use immediately."

> **–Stacey Rudnick** | Director, Center for Leadership & Ethics at the McCombs School of Business, The University of Texas at Austin

"*Leadership Unchained* is the book for leaders who are looking for new strategies and tactics to cope with the shifting ground of missed opportunities and unexpected threats in today's competitive and ever-changing environment…It's a must-read."

> **–Sylvia Acevedo** | CEO, Author, Engineer, Entrepreneur, Rocket Scientist

Leadership
UNCHAINED

Defy Conventional Wisdom for
BREAKTHROUGH
PERFORMANCE

Sara Canaday

T&C Press
Austin, Texas

Published by:

T&C PRESS

Austin, Texas
(512) 343-7991

Printed in the United States of America.

Content Development and Editing:
Susan Priddy (www.SusanPriddy.com)

Cover Design and Interior Layout:
Kendra Cagle (www.5LakesDesign.com)

Library of Congress Control Number: 2019930342

ISBN: 978-0-9846591-5-9 (paperback)
          978-0-9846591-6-6 (Kindle)
          978-0-9846591-7-3 (ePub)

Sara Canaday
sara@saracanaday.com
www.saracanaday.com

Table of Contents

INTRODUCTION

PUSH BACK
against the **OLD RULES**

What if the leadership practices we've worked so hard to master are now getting in the way? In fact, what if they are actually holding us down and preventing us from leading for growth and innovation?

Forget "what if." **It's happening.**

The rules for leadership success haven't just changed. They've radically evolved to accommodate a modern business landscape that's strangely fluid and requires a more nuanced approach for competing at a higher level.

> *The traditional, etched-in-stone wisdom that molded leadership for years has become increasingly less effective.*

In some cases, it's even impeding progress for the most talented professionals. For those who've always relied on conventional approaches to achieve superior performance, this new reality may be shocking.

Think about that.

Business experts and behavioral scientists identified the guiding principles for effective leadership, and many of us worked hard to perfect those competencies. We learned them. We applied them. We practiced them. We programmed our brains and our behaviors to take the well-worn path of what worked in the past. It was a simple, direct equation that consistently got results.

But now the leadership role is experiencing a metamorphosis. Its tried-and-true competencies are being tested (and sometimes even crushed) in our chaotic, digitally connected, globally competitive world. In the context of this new business environment, the old rules simply don't have the same impact.

So what's the solution?

Unfortunately, it's not as simple as throwing out the old competencies and learning new ones. It's about recognizing which approach will maximize our performance in a particular situation.

> *We need to develop the insights to know when to follow the conventional leadership rules — and when to break them.*

The key is learning to become more selective about the leadership behaviors we apply.

Sometimes the traditional approach is still the right choice. In other cases, we can strategically improve team performance by flipping those common habits upside down and taking the exact opposite action. Breaking the rules. Pushing back against the norms. Intentionally rewiring our thought processes to follow an unexpected route toward leadership success.

I'll be the first to admit: It's tough to un-do all that repetitive brain-muscle-memory. The leadership habits we've already formed are deeply ingrained. The behaviors and patterns have likely become automatic. Almost involuntary. And we've probably been recognized and rewarded for them at some point in our careers. Those habits are extremely sticky. For good reason.

No way around it, change isn't easy.

> *Breaking free from our old approach to leadership takes courage and discipline, but it's well worth it.*

And rest assured, there are exceptionally strong incentives for rebooting that leadership competency database in our brains.

The evidence? Just think about the envelope-pushing leaders in the news who are already daring to demonstrate unconventional success habits. They are confidently taking their companies into the future with bold, innovative, profit-boosting decisions that are redefining leadership for the next generation.

They know the old rules. They even use the old rules. But they aren't afraid to suddenly shake things up with a counterintuitive, almost paradoxical move when it gives them an advantage. They have learned how to break free from habitual practices to produce breakthrough results.

If you're a current or future leader, this book can become your game-changing guide to the new era of modern leadership – the kind that's no longer tethered to standard operating procedures and not afraid to redefine the rules.

In the chapters that follow, you'll learn to recognize the **chains that bind us** and the reasons they may be blocking your forward progress.

You'll discover **solutions to break free** from those chains and the new habits that are catapulting by-the-book leaders into modern thinkers.

Plus, you'll explore **strategies for breakthrough performance** that will help you incorporate the powerful, new rules for leadership success.

As you read in the pages ahead about the modern leaders who are bravely forging this new competency trail, you'll see the pure genius hidden within their dare-me-to-defy-conventional-wisdom approach.

And if you learn to apply those valuable insights?

You'll have a real advantage in navigating today's ultra-complex business landscape with its constantly evolving innovations. You'll be better equipped to take on new challenges in delightfully unexpected ways. And with each step, you'll dramatically increase your odds to produce extraordinary results.

Let go of your dependence on the old rules.

It's your turn to break free.

This is
LEADERSHIP UNCHAINED.

CHAPTER ONE

"I can't just sit here. I have to do something."

———————

SHAKE OFF
the **AGE-OLD BIAS** for Action

As humans, we are wired to get things done. The natural bias for action is in our DNA. It's strongly valued by our society. Heavily reinforced by prominent leaders.

It's an incredibly powerful influence, and I've seen it firsthand.

A major tech company brought me in to coach some of their executives during an outdoor business simulation at a Leadership Retreat. These leaders were participating in a complex scavenger hunt that involved a collaborative, problem-solving session in a natural trail setting.

One more thing: It was also a timed competition.

> *Imagine these extremely driven, highly ambitious executives competing for bragging rights.*

The participants were divided into several small groups, and each team was provided with a map, a compass, and a set of clues. The objective of the challenge was to follow the clues and earn points based on the level of difficulty in reaching the destination.

My role was to observe the communication patterns and behaviors within one of the groups during the event. I was only allowed to observe and couldn't provide any type of assistance.

Before the challenge started, my team of executives had three hours to discuss the most productive and efficient way to complete the task. As part of their operation plan, they defined roles, established responsibilities, and set outcome goals to satisfy the key stakeholders. They even elected a "map guru" and a "hint interpreter" to take the lead in solving directional challenges on the trail.

Without getting into the weeds, I can tell you that one element of their strategy involved the team members staying together when they received a clue to leverage the combined brain power of the group.

As all of the executives gathered anxiously at the starting line, the whistle blew, and the clock began ticking. My group quickly huddled up to read the first clue. Before most of the team members even finished reading the last line, one executive was convinced that his instincts were correct and darted off to the trees on the left. Another raced toward a dense set of bushes on the right, fully believing that her interpretation was accurate. The rest of the team followed suit and scattered frantically.

Immediate action. No brainstorming. No communication. Needless to say, abandoning the strategy (and the compass) was probably the least effective way to compete.

After finishing about one-third of the course, the team started to realize the error. If they wanted to be successful, they needed to stick together. To carefully re-read the hints. To rely on the compass. To patiently wait for the leader to point them in the right direction.

Once they reverted to their original strategy, the pace and manner in which they solved the clues started to improve. They became faster and more efficient at deciphering the hints, and their team synergy produced striking results.

This process was a key topic of discussion during our debriefing session. In hindsight, they could see how the competitive adrenaline rush and the time pressure ignited their natural bias for action. In the heat of the moment, they felt compelled — even *obligated* — to DO SOMETHING. To dive in and make it happen. Forget the strategy. Ditch the plan.

> *The need to act was like an uncontrollable reflex they couldn't stop, even though it wasn't according to plan and it was sabotaging their performance.*

One by one, they tried to explain this overwhelming urge to take action, and the underlying theme was the same: They just didn't feel like they were making a contribution to the team by standing still.

Take that in for a moment.

I have seen this same phenomenon with leaders in all types of organizations. Big companies. Start-ups. Non-profits. Government agencies. The habit of hair-trigger action has become standard operating procedure.

The perception tells the story. People who take action are seen as strong, disciplined, respected and successful. Those who don't? They are quickly classified as lazy or lacking in drive and ambition. The undeniable message comes through, loud and clear: If we want to succeed, we need to act.

The reinforcement goes even deeper. As professionals, we are often rewarded for our ability to take action and get things done. It's a habit that organizations cultivate in their high potentials and reward in their top executives. At any level of the organization, corporate action-takers are considered valuable assets. But as we have seen, that conventional wisdom has some serious faults.

Chains That
BIND US

Leaders who constantly allow the bias for action to reroute their schedules and thought processes will end up feeling tethered to the madness of "more."

The pressure to "do more" is quickly intensifying.

The *natural* tendency for action has been *unnaturally* elevated in today's fast-isn't-fast-enough business environment. Greater competition. Increased market complexity. Shorter product life cycles.

The expectations associated with action as a catalyst for success have exponentially increased. Leaders are now feeling pressure in unimaginable ways, as the bias for action has morphed into a bias for frenzy.

Think about how that happened.

The 24-hour news cycle has amplified the impression of incessant busy-ness. Social media has created the perceived obligation to be perpetually connected.

The promises of greater efficiency that came with our technological breakthroughs have actually fed an addiction to constant accessibility. At the end the day, all of us are left with the distinct impression that action isn't enough. To keep pace with the rest of the world, we need continuous action…and continuous acceleration.

Somewhere along the line, success became synonymous with the high-velocity momentum that results from strategic multi-tasking and the amped-up, hyper-fueled task of always doing more.

But let's be honest. That's completely exhausting and, at some point, impossible. It's as though the inherently positive bias for action got wildly stretched out of shape and, sadly, lost its purpose.

Action for the sake of action doesn't produce results.

One of the best examples of this can be found in a famous study published in the *Journal of Economic Psychology*. The researchers studied videotapes of goalkeepers playing in top soccer leagues and championships worldwide. Specifically, they analyzed 286 penalty kicks to determine the probability distribution of kick direction and the responses by these elite players.

The scientists discovered that the overwhelmingly optimal strategy for goalkeepers is to remain in the center of the net during the penalty kick. By NOT moving, they have a 33% chance of blocking the ball. Diving to the left only works 14.2% of the time, compared with 12.6% on the right. Seems like a no-brainer to wait in the middle during the kick to increase the odds of success.

But guess what? Statistically speaking, goalkeepers only stay in the center *about 6% of the time.*

Researchers were startled by that. Why would these highly experienced athletes deliberately undermine their own efforts to succeed?

As it turned out, the driving factor was the emotional impact of the response.

The players reported that they would *feel better* about missing the ball if they were moving the wrong way rather than standing frozen in the middle. They didn't want to appear lazy or look like they weren't trying.

Even though they recognized that moving from the center would significantly reduce their chances for success, they felt the overwhelming need to move. It was an emotional, visceral response rather than a logical one. They viewed DOING SOMETHING as preferable to DOING NOTHING, despite the consequences.

> *In other words, the bias for action was propelling them to behave in unproductive ways.*

That same phenomenon can be seen in the workplace environment. Leaders have developed an emotional trigger that subconsciously compels them to DO SOMETHING. In their minds, taking action feels like the best response: the correct, normal, proper, and successful thing to do. Even when it's not. The executives on the Leadership Retreat were a perfect example.

Leaders are expected to produce more innovation, more often.

At the same time leaders are feeling the pressure to take action at the dizzying pace of business, they are also expected to be more innovative and visionary. Organizations are feeling the heat of intense competition, so they push their leaders to rev up everything related to planning and strategy development. All the time. The foot never comes off the gas.

The dilemma is apparent. All of these big-picture-thinking activities require the time and, more importantly, the "mental space" to ponder the alternatives and envision vastly different solutions.

Essentially this establishes starkly competing goals: Leaders today are expected to simultaneously act more and think more.

As you might guess, that's completely unrealistic. The equation doesn't work. There's actually a high probability that more action will lead to less thinking. Which is a significant business problem when innovation is at a premium.

For years, researchers have studied the creative process in an effort to determine why some intelligent people come up with revolution-ary ideas and others don't. What is it that enables (or smothers) the inventive spirit?

They found that many components come into play during the pro-cess. But the common factor found among creative people who succeed is that they take time for their minds to wander.

Sounds completely counterintuitive, doesn't it? But it works.

They stop pushing themselves to robotically produce and allow the time to process experiences, sort information, reinforce learning, and reflect on setbacks. Pausing to think actually makes them more innovative, effective, and productive. It's a distinct advantage that is totally lost if people give in to the coercion to keep doing more.

In my first book, *You — According to Them,* I refer to this as "Perpetual Doer Syndrome." It's more common than you might think, and it robs well-meaning, competent managers of being seen as visionaries and leaders.

The natural bias for action combined with the increased pressure to be more innovative is presenting leaders with an epic challenge. We have a finite amount of mental and physical resources, as well as the unfortunate but unescapable parameter of 24 hours in a day.

Our minds and bodies have limits. Expecting ourselves to succeed in the context of a constant, act-more, think-more, produce-more world is self-defeating, at best. Worst-case scenario? It could be disastrous. For our projects, our teams, and even our health.

That's the crux of the problem. While constant motion might look like success on the outside, it could actually be undermining our leadership efforts in enormous ways.

Solutions to
BREAK FREE

Successful leaders in the modern era seem to have adopted a new habit — an unexpected one that involves pushing back against the deeply rooted bias for action.

Modern leaders have perfected the strategic pause.

Instead of making action the default for every challenge, these leaders are pairing that alternative with an opposite response. It's not about *replacing* action, which we know is a necessary leadership ingredient. We still need to reach our goals, meet deadlines, and produce results. This is different.

They think of it as developing a *companion* habit that celebrates BEING rather than DOING. It involves a *strategic pause*. A mental time-out. Space for their brains to percolate. Whatever we call it, this new habit requires consistently taking some time away from the chaos of business to let ourselves think.

We all need time to mentally breathe. To plan and reflect. To give our brains a chance to process all of the knowledge we've been packing in. Pausing allows us to connect the dots between information in different ways and look at challenges from a fresh angle that we simply can't do when we're in constant motion.

> *No doubt about it, modern leaders have realized the extraordinary benefits of the strategic pause. They don't mistake motion for meaning.*

Neuroscientists at Washington University tested this theory by collecting brain-scan data from people who were busy doing mental tasks like math problems and word games. While the intense focus of these tasks caused spikes in some parts of the brain, it also caused declines in other parts.

These researchers ultimately found a background activity in the brain that, oddly enough, is much more active when people are sitting quietly in a room doing nothing. That's a pivotal finding.

They discovered that the "resting brain" is actually quite busy with absorbing and evaluating information, but we curtail that function when we allow the "active brain" to hijack all the mental energy. If we want creativity to flourish, we need to deliberately pause on occasion and allow that background process to take priority.

> *Maximum effectiveness and innovation start with...STOPPING. Pausing to rest and think and just "be." Surprising? You bet! Profitable? Absolutely!*

Top organizations worldwide are tapping into this wisdom, including the Walt Disney Company, General Mills, and Google. Instead of trying to push employees to do more, they regularly give them time to stop and think.

That decision isn't just about creating a cool corporate culture or reducing employee stress. Executives within these organizations have seen bottom-line benefits from this practice, ranging from higher performance and productivity to more innovative ideas. Greater mental space is an approach that pays off in dollars and cents.

So the message for leaders seems to be simple: *Take a break.* Sounds easy, right?

Not so much.

The bias for action is strong and stubborn.
And in leaders, the bias is industrial strength
and triple reinforced.

Implementing a strategic pause takes real discipline.

One of the biggest champions of this modern habit is Jeff Weiner, CEO of LinkedIn.

In his speeches and blogs, he often talks about the priceless value of uninterrupted focus and time to think. If leaders want to produce visionary, big-picture ideas, they need downtime for their brains to compile the information they've gathered and connect it in unusual ways. Even though it seems crazy to schedule "nothing," Weiner firmly believes it's an unmatched productivity tool and an important investment in leadership success.

I must admit I have experience with this challenge on a personal level. I'll be the first one to confess that my bias for action is...well, pretty intense. I've been accused of caring more about results than relationships and more about deliverables than discoveries. While those characterizations are most definitely not accurate, my pesky bias for action was sometimes known to send another message.

Once I realized the vital importance of slowing down to make stronger connections with people and ideas, I started consciously reminding myself to hit pause at appropriate times. To temporarily suspend my fascination with getting things done. To recognize the business value of taking a break.

Still today, I have to intentionally acknowledge that "being" some-times trumps "doing" — even when that seems horribly off task for a high-energy, get-'er-done kind of gal. Let's just say that I continue to be a work in progress.

Modern leaders are selective about applying the new rule.

The most complicated part of this unconventional habit is knowing exactly when to apply it. Honoring the need for action but discern-ing when that's counterproductive. It's about knowing when to move forward and when to step back. Not procrastinating. Not rushing in. But recognizing when action is strategically advantageous and when it's not.

Organizational psychology expert Adam Grant highlighted this sub-ject in a TED talk, presenting a classic study that explored the concept of first-mover advantage. In business, we put a premium on being first to market. Beating our competitors with new product features. Racing to grab market share. The broad perception is that first-movers win the race.

But is that really true?

The researchers analyzed more than 50 product categories and com-pared the success of the "first-movers" who created the market versus the "improvers" who took the original idea and made it better.

The results were eye-opening: The failure rate of the first-movers was 47%, compared with 8% for the improvers.

Grant's brilliant take-away was this: Success isn't about being first; it's more about being different and better.

For these companies, pausing to think something through before diving in gave them a definitive edge.

Does that mean we should never be pioneers who lead the way? No! But we need to hone the ability to detect when it's more profitable to follow rather than blaze the new trail on our own. Finding that balance between rushing in and waiting is the sweet spot that allows leaders and their companies to achieve greater success.

Strategies for
BREAKTHROUGH PERFORMANCE

To elevate the quality of your leadership, learn when to break free from your bias for action. These guidelines will help you incorporate this new habit:

 Deliberately hit "pause."

Set time aside every day (or at least every week) to give yourself the mental space you need to become more productive. Allow time for creativity. For the neurons in your brain to connect in unusual ways. It can help you gain remarkable clarity and think about challenges on a bigger, broader level.

Become intentional about BEING rather than just DOING. More specifically, seek out the perfect balance between acting and thinking.

Not procrastinating or delaying without purpose. It's about pausing to strategize before moving forward at full speed. Find the equilibrium that provides your shortcut to success. Commit to it, and make it happen.

Yes, I know that will feel awkward at first. Your calendar is probably jam-packed with meetings and commitments, so it might seem unnecessarily selfish to mark off some "me time." Don't let that stop you. Consider this an unbreakable appointment with yourself.

Model this practice.

You already know that "doing nothing" has developed a bad reputation, so you can become one of the trailblazers who changes that perception. Remember: Your team members are closely watching how you act and react to every situation.

- *Demonstrate the value of the pause in your own career*

- *Be transparent with your team members about the need to step away and contemplate the alternatives*

- *Openly share with your employees the insights you gain from taking that downtime, explaining how those can benefit the team and the organization overall*

The added benefit to modeling the strategic pause is reinforcing your executive presence. Great leaders are known for their thoughtful, measured consideration rather than knee-jerk reactions and uncontrolled emotions. Taking time to think adds to the impression that you have the composure and confidence to make wise, well-reasoned decisions.

3 Encourage your team to pause.

As a leader, you have the power and influence to help your team members develop new habits that can make them more productive. Make sure they also have time in their schedules to stop and think. That's tricky when deadlines are tight, but the long-term benefits will be worth it. Give them the calendar space that encourages them to give it a try.

You'll probably discover that leaders aren't the only ones who are fighting the emotional tug to act rather than think. Just help your employees understand that it's a priority. An important part of meeting their individual achievements. It's up to you to guide them, insisting they occasionally hit the brakes to reflect on their progress and goals.

Leaders who can shake off the age-old bias for action and perfect the unconventional art of the strategic pause will reap a multitude of rewards. Mastering this ability — the nuanced judgment call of knowing when to pause and when to act — leads directly to greater productivity. Improved performance. Increased innovation. And measurable benefits.

CHAPTER TWO

"I have a great idea, and I know it will work!"

ESCAPE

from the Prison of
YOUR OWN PERSPECTIVES

Every year, the Museum at the Rhode Island School of Design in Providence hosts a fascinating program known as Docs and Cops.

This creative experiment uses artwork as a strategic tool to help people better understand others' viewpoints and expand their perspectives. As you might guess, the participants for the annual Docs and Cops event include approximately 10 physicians and 10 police officers. All highly skilled and extensively trained.

While these industries are distinctly different, the participants have all built their careers on the ability to quickly analyze complex situations and implement solutions that could have life-or-death consequences.

As the event begins, a trained guide leads these doctors and police officers silently through part of the museum to look at a selected group of paintings and sculptures. The small group discussions that follow are prompted by one primary question: What did you see?

After repeating this program for more than a decade, the organizers report it consistently sheds light on the thought-process variations of people in diverse occupations.

*In a nutshell? Their perceptions
are remarkably different.*

For instance, an abstract image that looks like a crime scene to detectives might be perceived as a collection of cells and neurons by the physicians. People in the same industry tend to notice the same types of details and, perhaps more importantly, ignore the ones that might seem significant to others.

So what does that prove? People can look at the exact same object and see something completely different. It's not about having dissimilar opinions or competing agendas. It's much bigger than that. Our actual vision is subconsciously filtered through the lens of our own unique experiences and perspectives.

Putting it another way, what we know shapes what we see.

Chains That
BIND US

The realization that we each have an inescapably tinted view of the world has enormous implications for leaders — and not necessarily in a good way.

Leaders bring their unique perspectives to the decision-making process.

No matter how objective and rational leaders try to be, they don't think in a vacuum. Just like the docs and cops, they look at every challenge and choice through the lens of their own perspectives, experiences and beliefs, which can easily impact the quality of their decisions.

This culprit is known as cognitive bias, defined as "a mistake in reasoning, evaluating, remembering, or other cognitive process, often occurring as a result of holding on to one's preferences and beliefs regardless of contrary information."

You can probably imagine all the ways cognitive bias creeps in to leaders' day-to-day thinking. As they size up any new situation, they instantly make judgments (good or bad) about an opportunity or a person. They base their gut instincts and intuition on previous successes and failures, using what they know to be true to extrapolate a theory. It's just not possible to "unring the bell" and forget what they already know.

Leaders are susceptible to emotional influences.

When it comes to taking risks, the emotional component can frequently outweigh all evidence to the contrary. Truthfully, emotions may play a bigger role in decision-making than spreadsheets and forecasts.

Ever been to a football game when the coach tells the team to go for it on fourth down with 8 yards to go in the first quarter — even though logic, statistics, and the angrily booing crowd indicate that's a phenomenally awful idea? Emotions can quickly hijack the decision-making process.

Maybe the coach wants to demonstrate to his players that he trusts them. Perhaps the media have been criticizing him for overly conservative play-calling, and he wants to prove them wrong. Or maybe he is longing for a chance to engineer an epic play that loyal fans recount for years to come. Hopes, desires, and emotions frequently blur the facts of reality.

The same thing happens in business: Decisions are never cut and dried. If leaders don't acknowledge that their decision processes begin from a non-neutral position and are constantly subjected to non-analytic influences, they can set their teams up for a major loss.

Leaders want to confirm their own ways of thinking.

One type of cognitive bias in particular tends to plague leaders, and American business guru Warren Buffett described it succinctly:

"What the human being is best at doing is interpreting all new information so that their prior conclusions remain intact."

Buffett is referring to the impact of something known as confirmation bias.

Leaders develop a hunch or an educated guess about the best way to solve a problem, and they set out full force to find information that will confirm their theory.

As they search, they place greater value on facts that agree with their positions while they tend to discount those that don't. Consciously or unconsciously. We see what we want to see.

After individuals form an opinion, they naturally gravitate toward sources that will confirm and reinforce their thinking. It's the same reason why many Democrats watch CNN and Republicans tune in to Fox News. People are simply more comfortable hearing information that supports their views and being in the presence of those who agree with them. It's human nature. We want to bask in the confirmation that our own approach is correct.

Unfortunately, that tendency has some serious drawbacks for leaders who are trying to make big decisions about things such as major investments or radical changes in their business operations. If they selectively block out the opposing views (even without realizing they are doing it), they may miss something vitally important. And what they don't see could possibly lead to lost opportunities or much, much worse.

Collaboration isn't always enough.

Many leaders today have read volumes of research that definitively supports the practice of collaboration — *bringing together people who see things differently to solve problems*. No doubt about it, collaboration amplifies the powerful synergy of teamwork.

For example, a 2017 article in *Forbes* described the results of a Stanford University study that measured the value of collaboration. Research participants who were involved with collaboration stuck with their tasks 64% longer than their peers who were working alone. The study also showed that collaboration was responsible for greater engagement, lower fatigue, and more successful performance.

What leader wouldn't love that?

In response to some of the earlier findings about collaboration, progressive companies such as Google and Apple quickly took action to reap those rewards. They led the way in completely redesigning their office spaces to create collaborative wonderlands with wide-open floor plans and group seating. They literally broke down the barriers between employees to provide more transparency and intimacy in hopes that the right environment would inspire greater collaboration and, in turn, greater innovation.

Was that effective? Many times, yes.

But here's the problem. As more and more companies jumped on the collaboration bandwagon, some leaders started to miss the point.

Productive collaboration requires more than simply gathering a big group of people around a table. That's only half of the equation.

Without the presence of truly diverse thinking that challenges ideas and pushes the creative envelope, collaboration becomes a watered-down, just-going-through-the-motions exercise.

Cognitive diversity is the real key. And when it's missing, it undermines a team's ability to succeed at the highest level.

The fact is, most teams today are much more homogeneous than people believe. So what's really behind that?

Knowingly or unknowingly, many managers "recruit in their own image." They want to add staff members whom they believe will seamlessly integrate with the other employees in their groups. They search for people who will be "on the same page" to efficiently get things done and meet tight deadlines.

Even when companies follow best practices in hiring demographically diverse people, some common characteristics will ultimately still exist within each employee population. Plus, the longer these employees work together under the same roof (physical or metaphorical), the more their spheres of experience overlap and their distinctive thought processes shrink.

Bottom line? Sometimes collaboration isn't enough.

Leaders may falsely assume that just bringing together a group of people is the answer to their quest for greater innovation. They can provide employees with comfy bean-bag chairs for meetings, install futuristic conversation pods, or engage employees in discussions around a fancy coffee bar. But if all the people involved are generally like-minded, the results will fall short.

Without cognitive diversity, collaboration is just an illusion.

Solutions to
BREAK FREE

Leaders who are willing to take a new path — one that departs from their own perspectives — are discovering a profitable differentiator.

Modern leaders constantly challenge their own thinking.

Successful leaders continuously remind themselves that cognitive bias is silently at work in the back of their minds. They know that their own decision-making doesn't come from a neutral position, so they push themselves to uncover other angles. Not a polite, obligatory surveying of the crowd to reach consensus, but a mold-breaking, eyebrow-raising exploration to prove themselves WRONG.

Sounds crazy, doesn't it?

> *Rather than searching for sources and opinions that support their ideas, these leaders make a radical choice to go in the exact opposite direction.*

They actively seek out perspectives that will *discredit* their own thinking. It's a decisive, kick-confirmation-bias-to-the-curb move that takes many people by surprise, but it pays off.

One way that leaders are actively pursuing diverse, even diametrically opposed, viewpoints is by working to understand the people on their teams (in-house or beyond) who approach problems from the opposite direction. Making the effort to see things through their eyes could help leaders extend their thinking beyond the usual boundaries.

That was the exact challenge facing leaders in the education industry in 2000, when K-12 teachers began to notice that students born after 1980 simply didn't seem as engaged in the classroom material. The typical solution would have involved updating the curriculum or purchasing new textbooks.

Instead of doing what had always worked, industry leaders were willing to stretch and try to understand the different perspectives of this new generation to better meet their goals.

In 2001, an educational consultant named Marc Prensky confirmed striking differences in the brain function of people born into a world where the Internet and digital communications have always existed. These students look at life from a completely different perspective. He coined the term "digital natives" to describe this generation, versus the previous one he referred to as "digital immigrants."

To achieve success with these digital natives, educators had to stop thinking that their traditional teaching approach was the only one with value. They sought to understand this different perspective through testing, surveys, focus groups, observations, and elaborate teaching simulations. These educators proved that they wanted to see the world from the digital natives' viewpoint.

Today, many teachers are creatively integrating technology in the classroom to accelerate and support learning. Their lesson plans now accommodate information that students can access using smartphones, laptops, and tablet computers. More schools have switched to digital textbooks, which will eventually become standard issue. These types of changes have increased engagement and transformed the way students assimilate knowledge in the 21st century.

That positive transformation would never have been possible if educators weren't willing to push themselves and re-think some of what they do to accomplish their goals.

In the business world, successful leaders do the same thing. They acknowledge that some people are simply wired in a different way but their ideas and perspectives are equally valuable. These leaders confidently search to find what's missing. They refuse to settle for the obvious. And they consistently challenge their own views in the pursuit of stronger and more innovative solutions.

Modern leaders leverage the benefits of strategic collaboration.

Today's most successful leaders aren't content to sleepwalk through the bleary-eyed process of half-hearted collaboration. They wake it up (and shake it up!) with a triple espresso shot of different perspectives.

> *Cognitive diversity isn't an option for them;*
> *it's a daily, relentless pursuit.*

Regina Dugan, former VP of Engineering at Facebook, described this approach in a *Fast Company* article, calling cognitive diversity the most powerful tool in business:

> *"We (all) want to make things that haven't been made before, and that's tremendously exciting. It's exhilarating, it's invigorating, and it's hard. Cognitive diversity is absolutely the key to innovation. When we are working on very difficult problems, it's essential to have different voices in the room. On my teams, it is common to see Oscar-winning directors working side-by-side with coders, or physicists working with textile manufacturers."*

Leaders such as Dugan have adopted the new approach of strategic collaboration to ensure their teams are representing a full range of ideas and perspectives. They purposely seek out cognitive diversity to solve tough challenges.

From a realistic standpoint, strategic collaboration requires confidence, patience, and a long-term view of success.

Why? Bringing together a wildly diverse group of people to provide their distinct opinions is not the recipe for short, simple, conflict-free meetings. Nope. Most definitely not.

Odds are, these participants will be opinionated and actively stirring the pot. Strategic collaboration is almost guaranteed to incite some lively, passionate disagreements among team members. But leaders use it anyway, and they know it will be effective.

These leaders are willing to welcome a process that is sometimes a little more messy — maybe even uncomfortable — to generate the best possible ideas and approaches that will help the company achieve greater success in the long term.

Steve Miller, former CEO of Shell Oil Co., was well known for his use of strategic collaboration. As Shell was rebranding in Europe, he invited a group of employees to join him on an unusual bus tour.

The invitees? People from accounting, IT, marketing, operations, engineering, and administration. Company veterans and new hires representing 25 countries. That's some serious cognitive diversity right there!

Traveling together, this unlikely crew visited many of the organization's retail locations to observe and provide feedback. In between stops, they'd climb back on the bus to talk about what they saw.

Miller knew that everyone in the group had physically looked at the same thing, but they all saw something different. The engineers started talking about pump capacity and customer safety issues. The marketing people discussed the impact of signage and point-of-sale promotions inside the store. The IT people had questions about the cash register software and its ability to wirelessly sync with the product-inventory database.

The end result?

Bringing together people with these vastly different perspectives provided a richer, deeper view of the organization's business function.

This exercise required time and money, but it generated priceless, holistic input that catapulted the company forward rather than moving a few inches at a time.

Another interesting example of strategic collaboration actually comes from someone who was way, way ahead of his time on this approach.

Abraham Lincoln had been involved in a bitter fight for the Republican presidential nomination leading up to the 1860 election. His rivals were extremely vocal about their differences, and the process became quite divisive. But after Lincoln won the nomination and eventually became President, he made what was, at the time, a head-scratching choice.

He realized America was facing tremendous challenges, and the country's survival was dependent on leadership by the most intelligent, outspoken people. He knew that wouldn't happen with a Cabinet full of "yes men" who shared his views. He needed to find trusted collaborators with different perspectives – even opposing ones – who were willing to speak up for the good of the country. He wasn't looking for harmony; he was looking for innovative thinkers.

Despite the bad blood from the primary election, Lincoln acknowledged that his former rivals were smart, savvy men who shared his deep love for America. In a move that shocked everyone, Lincoln appointed these men to top positions on his new team. Missouri Attorney General Edward Bates became the U.S. Attorney General, Ohio Governor Salmon Chase was appointed Secretary of the Treasury, and New York Senator William Seward was named Secretary of State.

I'm guessing the first Cabinet meeting was more than a little awkward, as these fierce competitors had to make the mental switch to become teammates. But Lincoln believed so strongly in the benefits of strategic collaboration that he was willing to endure that discomfort and make the country's needs a priority.

Successful business leaders do the same for their companies.

Modern leaders hire for cognitive diversity.

Recruiting is a complicated process, and it usually occurs on a fairly tight time frame. Modern leaders are taking the extra steps to make sure the people who join their teams truly represent diverse perspectives that can help accelerate their organizations' success.

A thriving company in the Silicon Valley takes that message to heart.

IDEO, an international design and consulting firm, is legendary because of its long history of award-winning, off-the-charts innovation. The organization operates according to a consistent principle: *"Creativity occurs at the intersection of different perspectives."*

That principle explains why a company developing highly technical products and services hires people with oddly diverse backgrounds. The IDEO employee roster has the usual list of engineers, industrial designers and MBAs, but also people with degrees in history, music, and medicine.

The organization demonstrates its core belief that people from different backgrounds bring much more to the table than their primary career skills. They also provide diverse thought processes that spur imaginative product development in unprecedented ways. For IDEO, hiring for cognitive diversity is a strategy that definitely works.

It takes genuine self-confidence for leaders to recruit and hire employees with vastly different viewpoints, but their efforts are routinely rewarded. By consciously building teams of diverse thinkers, modern leaders are increasing their odds for success.

Strategies for
BREAKTHROUGH PERFORMANCE

If you sense that your team could benefit from an infusion of fresh perspectives, make the choice to apply these new rules. The steps that follow can give you a jumpstart:

 ## Fight back against cognitive bias.

Recognize that your thoughts and opinions come with a natural slant. It's always there. You can't compartmentalize enough to erase the past experiences and current emotions that ever-so-slightly color your view.

To combat that, make it a habit to challenge your thinking. Look past information that confirms your own theories to search for facts that might refute them.

Ask yourself some key questions to help you move toward decision-making from a more neutral position:

- *Do I automatically approach challenges the way I always have in the past?*

- *Do I start from the beginning to solve a problem or do I approach it with underlying assumptions?*

- *Do I jump to conclusions about whether an idea will or won't work?*

- *What am I not seeing? What's missing?*

- *Do I consider that my ideas and perspectives might be wrong or out of date?*

- *Is there information that can discredit my idea or approach?*

- *Have I put myself in a position to see things through a different lens?*

- *Do I customarily discuss situations with people who see things differently than I do (or flat-out disagree with me)?*

- *Am I willing to seek out other opinions before I determine a solution?*

2 Become a champion of strategic collaboration.

Remind yourself that collaboration isn't the same thing as *strategic collaboration*. When you make active, purposeful choices to assemble cognitively diverse teams, you'll get strikingly different results.

If you were gathering a group to help plan a customer advisory panel or customer appreciation event, your first inclination might be to include representatives from Sales and Marketing. Break that mold!

Bring in some analytical thinkers to balance the creative types, perhaps adding committee members from finance or engineering. Choose people who have attended the event in previous years, along with some who are newcomers with no preconceived notions. Factor in different ages, different cultural backgrounds, and different types of expertise.

Make it a priority to bring together people who offer diverse perspectives, ideas, and thought processes. Stay focused on the end goal. It's not always the easiest approach, but you can trust that strategic collaboration will deliver a measurable competitive edge.

 Diversify your team portfolio.

Set a goal to hire for *cognitive diversity.* Expand the parameters of your recruiting process to search for people who will deliberately challenge the thinking of your teams.

Of course, you still need to hire employees who check all the right boxes in terms of skills, experience, and credentials. But be deliberate about adding one more box: the ability to view problems from a completely different angle and contribute new perspectives. The potential impact on your team could be remarkable.

Over time, those wise hiring decisions will provide your team with valuable insights that would have otherwise been missing. And, better yet, these diverse thinkers will increase the potential of your organization to grow and compete at an exponential rate.

 Constantly seek input from "perspective-expanders."

Even when you create a cognitively diverse team, the shared scope of experiences and common corporate culture will slowly make the group become more homogeneous. It's up to you, as the leader, to crash the complacency and bring in envelope-pushing concepts from people and sources outside of your team and your organization.

How can you incorporate more perspective-expanders into your leadership realm?

- *Invite other leaders to your staff meetings to share what they are working on. That will prompt you and your team to think and strategize beyond the confines of your functional concerns.*

- *Network with colleagues outside of your industry who can give you access to different approaches and ideas. Interact regularly with people who will challenge you. Even disagree with you. Don't shy away from that; pursue it.*

- *Engage with a mastermind group comprised of people from other career paths who will candidly express diverse ideas and constructive criticism. What can you learn from these boundary-pushing interactions?*

- *Read books, blogs, and articles by unlikely sources who represent the polar opposite of your thinking and attitudes. What lessons could you apply?*

- *Take the lead in becoming the perspective-expander for your team after you've gathered these counterintuitive insights from outside sources. Challenge your employees to think in unexpected ways and approach problems differently – maybe even in reverse. Inspire them to find connections between seemingly unconnected elements.*

When you enthusiastically take on your role as a thought leader and perspective-expander, you have the opportunity to disrupt business as usual and completely change the game for your organization.

———————————

Modern leaders have learned to escape from the prison of their own perspectives. They aren't just finding success through an openness to new ideas; they passionately seek them out. They value cognitive diversity and invite team members to prove them wrong. They let go of the need to validate their own perspectives and focus all of their energy on finding the best solution to meet shared goals. No matter where those solutions might originate.

CHAPTER THREE

"The numbers never lie."

DITCH

the Need to Let Hard Data
DRIVE EVERY DECISION

In 2009, Nokia was the world's largest cell phone manufacturer. A woman named Tricia Wang was working in the company's research department at the time, and she held the position of Technology Ethnographer. Similar to a cultural anthropologist, Wang's job was to identify market trends and potential new customers by analyzing the qualitative side of human behavior related to cell phone usage.

Wang was specifically assigned to study the preferences and habits of low-income consumers in China. To say that she immersed herself in this task is putting it mildly.

She spent several years living with Chinese migrants, and she worked as a street vendor selling dumplings. She observed and interacted daily with people in neighborhood Internet cafes. She asked questions, and she listened to the answers. *Really* listened. Reading between the lines to capture the emotions and subtext lurking below the surface of their verbalized responses.

Using a boots-on-the-ground approach, she gathered a wide range of profound personal insights directly from these people. Through her many conversations with the locals, Wang discovered something she didn't anticipate.

Despite their very limited incomes, many Chinese people were so enamored with the new "smartphones" that they would sacrifice half of everything they earned in a month to have one. And those who didn't have smartphones desperately wanted one. The demand was enormous — and completely unexpected in this demographic group.

Essentially, Wang had uncovered a massive, hidden market for affordable smartphones.

Wang enthusiastically shared this great news with Nokia executives, who quickly responded with a polite, "Thanks, but no thanks." Their extensive quantitative research with millions of data points was driving a clear strategy to produce full-featured smartphones for high-end users.

In their opinions, Wang's qualitative data and small sample size didn't measure up to the mountain of numbers they'd already collected.

Fast forward a few years, and you'll see that Nokia paid a huge price for ignoring Wang's recommendation. Looking at the numbers alone sent them down the wrong road with their brand strategy. In 2012, the company ended up losing $4 billion and, ultimately, was forced to sell off its phone business to Microsoft.

Leaders in all types of companies run the risk of making this same, tragic error in judgment. They tend to value the measurable more than the unmeasurable. They get blinded by the numbers and the statistics, so they miss out on the human insights behind them that actually drive sales and revenue.

Chains That
BIND US

A number of key factors contribute to leaders' risky practice of over-relying on hard facts.

Leaders are drowning in data.

"Big Data" is a really big deal today. That's understandable, considering leaders depend on detailed information to make informed business decisions.

It's actually mind-boggling to think about all the data that can be collected and compiled using advanced software, sophisticated algorithms, and enormous databases. With a few clicks of the mouse, leaders can access extraordinarily precise demographic break-downs. Detailed pricing projections linked directly to current eco-nomic forecasts. Specific metrics about everything from website clicks to help-desk response times.

Take a moment and consider the extraordinary depth and breadth of all this data.

> *According to global research firm IDC, the world's information doubles every two years. Every. Two. Years.*

Could you imagine what that would look like if it applied to all of the physical items in your office or your home? Six years from now, you wouldn't even be able to step in to these jam-packed, claustrophobia-inducing environments.

This astounding overabundance of information has the same impact on our mental space. Everything becomes crowded, cluttered, and confused. Which makes it hard to think, much less innovate and strat-egize in original ways.

To be clear, quantifiable information is a good thing. It's necessary. But here's the problem.

Big Data's power to measure virtually anything can become almost intoxicating. In some ways, it quietly fuels an endless obsession with data. The only way to maintain the "high" of quantification euphoria?

Collect more data. Do it faster. Slice it differently. And what if the numbers don't provide a clear direction? The go-to solution is typically to gather more data. The bias for action is alive and well!

There's a very real danger that leaders find themselves drowning in the sheer volume of spreadsheets, reports, and statistics. Analytics overload sets in like a thick, dense fog. And when that happens, it becomes impossible to determine what matters and, more importantly, what doesn't.

We don't always question the facts.

If we all took a poll today, I'm confident it would confirm this statement: Most leaders tend to value hard data over soft intelligence. With so many complex variables involved in business, decision-makers often gravitate to the comfort of the absolute. And why not? The numbers don't lie. Solid data is credible. Cold, hard facts are reassuring.

Think about that. Customers and investors don't cough up the cash based on a hunch or some strong feelings. They want to see an objective, measurable business case with proof. They trust the facts. Bring on the charts and graphs! When data enters the negotiation arena with its bullet-proof clout, the questions stop.

Here's the downside.

> *The underlying belief that people should rely on the facts without question stifles the unique creativity of strong leaders.*

They often bring to their jobs a depth of experience, rich insights, and strong instincts about customers or the market that's based on years of working in the industry. When organizations value the numbers above everything else, all of that beefy qualitative knowledge can get lost in the shuffle.

As long as the data collection occurs in a relatively sound manner, people just don't question the facts. It's a common habit that can create a major stumbling block for leaders.

Objective information has a subjective side.

Cort Dial is an entrepreneur, investor, and author of the excellent book, *"Heretics to Heroes."* He proved this concept about subjective data while facilitating a leadership retreat for a major corporation.

He selected four VPs to participate in an exercise and provided each one with a page of data to use independently in preparing a short presentation. The rest of the group would be asked to evaluate these presentations and decide (hypothetically) which of the VPs should be fired, promoted, or retained based on their performance.

No pressure, right?

You can probably imagine the enthusiasm that emerged from these highly competitive executives who did NOT want to lose this "game" in front of their colleagues and peers. When the speakers had finished and it was time for the vote, the room was filled with an awkward tension and some nervous laughter.

It wasn't easy to compare four presentations that were completely different in terms of style and content, especially knowing that the comparison would determine which VP would be kicked off the island, so to speak. Reputations and egos were involved here.

After the voting results were announced, the entire team joined in a lively discussion about the validity of their choices. That's when Cort stood up to make a surprising announcement.

The VPs who had delivered those four, distinctive presentations had all basically been given *exactly the same data* as a starting point. The samples were in varied formats and included some "statistical noise" that made them appear to be different, but the core information was identical.

These disguised differences made it possible for every VP to choose a different "headline" to feature and add their own personal slants on the key takeaways. Same information; vastly different outcome.

What does that mean in the real world beyond the leadership retreat?

> *Even the most objective information comes with a subjective slant.*

Leaders view data according to their own internal biases, attitudes, and perspectives. And, right or wrong, their decision to approve or reject data may also be related to the approach, charisma, and influence of the presenter.

Hard facts aren't as black and white as leaders might think they are and, sometimes, data can lead us astray.

Data may not tell the whole story.

When one of my normally energetic colleagues started experiencing overwhelming fatigue, her doctor ordered a wide range of bloodwork to determine the cause. It took every ounce of energy she had to drag herself to the follow-up appointment, where the doctor smiled and announced: *"Great news! All of your test results came back in the normal range. You are perfectly fine!"*

Needless to say, those numbers weren't telling the whole story. The same thing happened at Nokia — and it happens at businesses around the globe.

> *When leaders are armed with credible data, they may get a false sense of security that prevents them from searching for the real story behind the numbers.*

They neglect to explore the authentic customer experience. To understand the extenuating circumstances. To identify the exceptions to the rule. Leaders may be tempted to zoom in and hyper-focus on the meaty data, but they won't accurately capture the full picture and all its nuances without a wide-angled view of the situation.

Solutions to
BREAK FREE

Trailblazing leaders today have recognized the tendency to be held hostage by information overload. Even though it feels unnatural, they give themselves permission to break free from their dependence on data. Do they still value the facts? Definitely. They just work to gain a broader context about the meaning.

They're willing to be informed by data but not ruled by it.

Modern leaders embrace Whole Data.

Leaders who are open to the idea of Whole Data — a more comprehensive view of the facts — stretch beyond the usual quantitative boundaries to incorporate intangible elements about their customers as they plan for next steps.

They pay attention to stories and narratives, emotions and attitudes, worries and complaints, risks and vulnerabilities. They dig down to find the motivations behind customer decisions, and they identify how policies, processes, and products actually impact the lives of the people behind the statistics. They search for the qualitative information that paints a more vivid picture of the customer experience.

These leaders take a new approach.

They demonstrate the wisdom of integrating hard data and soft intelligence in the decision-making process to achieve superior results.

When a major U.S. airport decided to embark on a terminal redesign, the owners followed a Whole-Data approach rather than just sending out architects and designers to spruce up the space.

They spent time with passengers to determine what was really important to them. And guess what? When given a list of potential options that included fancy upgrades and concierge-type additions that might appeal to them, passengers and employees alike strongly preferred one amenity over everything else combined: *clean restrooms.*

That's what *really* mattered. Not fancy artwork or moving sidewalks or chic lighting.

Capturing that information in advance led the owners to a relatively inexpensive solution that had immediate and significant impact on customer satisfaction. Before construction ever started on the interior design upgrade, managers ordered an increase in the frequency and quality of bathroom cleanings and sanitation throughout the terminal.

By using a Whole-Data approach, the owners were able to more effectively prioritize the project and invest in what really mattered. And, by the way, it worked. This simple change contributed to tremendous accolades for the airport after it demonstrated the biggest jump in customer-experience rankings among U.S. airports in a single year.

Modern leaders aren't afraid to ask questions.

Making the decision to be driven by Whole Data rather than numbers alone requires a willingness to ask questions.

Early in my career, I worked for a large corporation that hired a management consulting firm to help with increasing efficiency. Representatives from this firm were brought in to complete a Time and Motion Study, which involved weeks of quietly observing sales representatives. They scribbled furiously on their clipboards as they documented how we spent our time and worked with call-in customers.

All of those observations were then compiled into a comprehensive (and likely expensive) final report that detailed our current level of productivity and recommendations for improvement.

While this thick report was packed full of elaborate graphs and bar charts, it was missing something very important. Not one of the representatives had ever asked any of us directly our opinions about the various processes and tools we used to do our jobs.

If they had only inquired, I would have told them that the clunky software format and the outdated service processes were the root of the problem. Serving a client on the phone was time-consuming and inefficient because we were toggling back and forth between different programs to find the information we needed.

No matter how prepared we were, it took an inordinate amount of time to find answers to customer questions. That was frustrating for us, as well as the customers, and projected an image of being disorganized.

We could have added great value to the overall findings of this study, but the representatives simply didn't ask.

Honestly, it's tough to venture into this territory. The facts seem so comfortable and familiar. But success in our current environment is now determined by leaders who are willing to step out of their comfort zones and ask tough questions beyond the realm of data. A British researcher named Graham Martin referred to this as pursuing "radical discomfort." I love that idea.

Modern leaders factor in their own experiences.

The other necessary component for leaders who rely on Whole Data is the willingness to factor in their own experiences and intuition.

> *They believe in their gut instincts and the relevance of the insights they've gained throughout their careers — sometimes even when the numbers don't agree.*

Steve Jobs was a perfect example of this concept. Reams of data and research indicated that tablet computers were a terrible idea. Jobs' instincts told him something different. Ultimately, he ignored the data and introduced the iPad, which completely changed the scope of the computing industry. Experts now predict that tablets will eventually outsell laptops all over the world.

Of course, trusting your gut doesn't always result in a billion-dollar win. Sometimes it's a big risk. But today's remarkably successful leaders remain open to the idea.

They understand that hard data has a subjective side, and they are motivated to find the rest of the story. They step out of their offices to talk with customers, vendors, colleagues, and employees. They aren't afraid to explore the feelings and emotions behind the statistics – and then they trust their instincts and experience to interpret those numbers accordingly.

Using that wisdom, they find real balance between the quantitative and the qualitative sides of the business-strategy coin.

Strategies for
BREAKTHROUGH PERFORMANCE

To begin breaking free from your habit of data dependence, try implementing these steps:

Change your mindset to value Whole Data.

I get it: This might require some serious effort if you're naturally wired to put all your trust in the facts. Force yourself to think outside the data box, and focus on the potential benefits. It will get easier – especially when you start reaping the rewards.

There's a proven, synergistic power that comes from integrating hard facts and soft intelligence. Instead of thinking that qualitative information somehow dilutes the quantitative, reframe the equation. Added together, these two different types of data actually create a stronger, more vivid picture of your opportunities.

It's like taking a black-and-white illustration and transforming it into a bright, glossy, full-color photograph. The more details you can see, the better your ability to make smart business decisions.

2 Adopt strategies for seeking out soft intelligence.

Recognizing the value of Whole Data isn't enough to harness its advantages. Be deliberate about pursuing it. Consider these tools as you create a system to methodically mine for soft intelligence within your organization:

- *Conduct customer focus groups on a regular basis to get direct feedback*

- *Interview potential customers at the point of purchase to understand how they are comparing your products or services with those of your competitors*

- *Observe customers using your products or services to uncover any hidden challenges or opportunities for improvement*

- *Expand your satisfaction surveys to ask about the reasons behind the ratings customers provide and try to determine what really matters to them*

- *Review transcripts from your call centers to look for patterns in the types of inquiries or complaints, as well as customer attitudes and tones*

Ask data-filtering questions.

As you work to elevate the quality of your decision-making with Whole Data, use these questions to guide the process:

- *Am I confident that this data reveals the entire picture? What might be missing?*

- *Does this view of the data include the human factor?*

- *Do I trust our field research? Is it up to date?*

- *Have I observed customers using our products and services in their natural habitats?*

- *Have I asked stakeholders directly how the data stacks up against their reality?*

- *Have I solicited stories from those impacted by the data?*

- *How are my own personal biases or presuppositions coloring my analysis?*

- *Am I dismissing the unmeasurable component out of habit?*

- *What conversations are we NOT having because we might be sidetracked by the data?*

 ## Find balance, and trust your gut.

If you've been intentional about gathering hard facts and soft intelligence, step back and take a look at that dynamic combination of information through the filter of your own experiences. Despite what the data reveals, your instincts may be telling you something different.

In some ways, that might seem unsettling. But remember this: Your unique knowledge of the customers and the markets may give you a clear view of the situation that can't be measured with a report or a focus group or a survey.

Never underestimate the insights you bring to the table. Instead of ignoring those, leverage them.

Just for the record, I'm not talking about nonchalant, ungrounded hunches reminiscent of a night in Vegas with someone screaming, "Double down, and bet it all!" That would be reckless. And it could likely end with some serious discussions about your judgment (or, worse yet, your employment).

I'm suggesting that you tap into the educated, rational intuition that has made you a successful leader in the past. Make the commitment to rely on Whole Data. Give equal attention to the quantitative and the qualitative, and get clarity on exactly what matters to your customers. How they think. What they need. Why they buy. Then go with your gut — not in a flippant, off-the-cuff way, but applying your plausible, data-informed instincts.

———————

Leaders who can ditch the need to let hard data drive every decision are discovering remarkable benefits. When they choose a balanced approach to information rather than over-relying on hard data, they are opening the door to unprecedented success.

CHAPTER FOUR

"But it's on my to-do list."

DROP

Your Dependence on
WHAT YOU'VE ALWAYS DONE

Ask any avid gardener: If you want to accelerate the growth of a tree, you have to prune it at the proper times. How's that for backwards logic? To make it grow bigger, you have to cut it back. Strange but true. Even essential.

Oddly enough, the same concept applies to leaders AND organizations.

> *If we want remarkable business growth, sometimes we need the courage to prune the proverbial tree.*

I recently found a wealth of information on that topic in a book by former CEO John Bell called *Do Less Better: The Power of Strategic Sacrifice in a Complex World*. Let's just say, Mr. Bell knows a thing or two about corporate pruning.

Nabob Foods Limited was a packaged foods company with a portfolio of items that ranged from desserts, jams, and peanut butter to coffees, teas, and spices. In 1977, the outlook for Nabob was bleak, with bankruptcy looming on the horizon. Costs were outpacing profits. Market share was down. Morale was even lower.

The owners knew the clock was ticking, and it was time for them to throw a "Leadership Hail Mary." In a desperate move to save the company, they hired John Bell as the VP of Marketing. Bell would have to make some tough decisions if he wanted to help the organization survive.

After analyzing the 12 product lines, Bell came to an important realization: Less is more. He wanted to pour all of the organization's investment and energy into the products that really mattered and could give the company a chance to turn around. Needless to say, this was a controversial move. Some of these brands had a long history and a loyal consumer following.

Initially, Nabob dissolved eight of its 12 products. Two more followed shortly after that. And suddenly, the general grocer emerged as a specialist in coffee (and, to some extent, tea).

The choice to let go had immediate consequences. The company's portfolio value dropped from $70 million to $40 million. One plant closed, and more than 300 jobs were eliminated. But, of course, the alternative was much worse.

After retraining employees to position themselves as coffee specialists, Nabob incorporated innovative, vacuum-sealed packaging and a dynamic advertising campaign that helped it compete with industry giants Kraft and Nestle. Within two years, the company had captured an astounding 25% of the Canadian coffee market.

Under the guidance of then-CEO John Bell, Nabob's profits soared. The thriving company was later purchased by Kraft in 1994.

It wasn't easy, but Nabob made the conscious effort to let go of the products that were draining the company and concentrate on the ones with the greatest potential for success. Without that strategic change, the organization would have likely closed its doors.

A similar phenomenon occurs with individual leaders who are facing complex challenges. Letting go is rarely the first inclination. But the constant and cumulative pressure to compete by always adding more has its limits – and its consequences.

Chains That
BIND US

Some of the regular habits and patterns established by leaders over time may have inadvertently become roadblocks.

Leaders develop strong attachments to their work.

One of the hallmarks of great leaders is the passion they demonstrate for the projects they own: the initiatives, services, products, functions, processes, or systems. They've championed them. Fought for them. Financed them. Maybe even cashed in some political capital to get them approved. It's safe to say that these leaders can become personally invested in the success of their work.

And why not? Being associated with a winning initiative that steadily contributed to the bottom line might have catapulted their careers. Or increased their perceived worth to the organization and its mission. What started out as a strategic venture aligned with corporate goals may have provided just as much "professional revenue" for the leaders themselves.

Another possibility is that leaders are simply programmed to believe that achieving more is directly related to doing more. If they aren't meeting their goals, they're NOT likely to think, *"What do I need to give up?"* Letting go might feel counterproductive – or perhaps even reckless. The natural tendency for these leaders is to hold on tight to the projects they have and seek out additional ones to help them hit their targets.

> *It's understandable that attachments form, whatever the reason behind it. But those attachments may get in the way of reaching a larger objective.*

If leaders are too committed to a sacred-cow project, product or service, the organization may end up with a wandering herd. Bottom line, a potential lack of objectivity in evaluating what's best for the business (and, more specifically, what may need to go, despite its success) can create major problems for leaders and for their companies.

It's tough to break out of the normal routine.

Leaders often rely on repeatable tasks to get more done during their time at the office. By putting some practices and functions on auto-pilot, they can reserve their brain power for more important things.

But there's also a snag. As they slide almost effortlessly into those familiar routines, they may be neglecting some critical questions. Namely, what do I need to *stop* doing?

Since I can remember, my father has followed the exact same pattern every time he stops to fill up his car with gasoline. Once the tank is full, he carefully removes the worn, leather binder from the glove compartment. He then logs in the mileage and gallons purchased so he can precisely calculate the car's efficiency in miles per gallon.

Here's the thing. According to Edmunds, 92% of vehicles made after 2011 can instantly display the average and current fuel economy with the click of a button. (Yes, my dad's car has that feature – and he is well aware of it!) Even though there's a faster and easier way to get the information he needs, he clings to this familiar habit rather than trying a new approach. It's just what he has always done. And hey, it still works!

Does it really matter if my dad wants to calculate his car's gas mileage the old-fashioned way? Of course not. But what happens if leaders are essentially doing the same thing? That's a vastly different story.

Think about all the deeply ingrained practices and tasks that leaders develop throughout their careers and rely on every single day. They pull up the same tired, old spreadsheets and update the numbers. They keep distributing the monthly report that no one is reading. They continue to use the outdated customer feedback because it is readily available.

All of those tasks can become part of the regular routine. Almost like background noise that is rarely noticeable, but always there.

> *Despite their best intentions, these leaders have inadvertently become chained to doing work that no longer adds value.*

Maybe there's a better way to do it. Or it's not even necessary, and they could use that time to work at a higher level.

Either way, these leaders are buried by their own recurring set of routine tasks. And here's the startling kicker: *They don't even realize they're suffocating.* The upshot is a serious drag on productivity and performance.

The to-do list can take on a life of its own.

Leaders can easily become slaves to their schedules if they automatically sanction everything on their calendars and to-do lists. Technology is making the problem even worse. Today's digital calendars make it oh-so-easy to add an entry and click that deceptively innocuous button marked "repeat."

The staff meeting is every Monday at 9:00. The budget update is always due on Wednesdays by 3:00. The account report has to be submitted before 5:00 every Friday. The list goes on. Quarterly employee evaluations. Annual reviews. Executive planning sessions. Detailed briefings for Sales and Marketing.

Before the week ever begins, leaders' to-do lists can become jam-packed with "mandatory" events and deadlines.

Even months in advance, their calendars are overflowing with wall-to-wall commitments and required tasks.

As if that doesn't provide enough frustration, there's a deeper layer to the problem. Leaders are presumably promoted or hired for their ability to add genuine value to the organization. However, they can't do that if they don't have time for the leadership activities that will set them apart. Strategic thinking. Long-term planning. Innovative brainstorming. Tasks that require the mental space and focused concentration to be effective.

I've coached many leaders who struggle with this impossible time crunch. They would strongly prefer to be more involved in the big picture of the business, but the demands and expectations of the daily grind keep them confined to a tactical box. And when leaders feel mentally bound to an overwhelming to-do list, those higher-level functions are the first to go.

Rationalization is seductively easy.

Perpetual to-do lists and routine tasks can certainly take their toll. But, rest assured, leaders are known for getting extremely creative with the art of rationalization. They can usually come up with brilliant and seemingly valid reasons to continue on the same path.

Do any of these comments ring a bell?

> *"Those staff meetings aren't very productive, but they do give the team members a chance to socialize. That's really important, too."*

> *"It will take too much time to canvass our users, and we have a deadline. Just gather the information from the system survey like we did last quarter. It's all the same anyway."*

> *"I can't cancel the review sessions with the salespeople. They EXPECT those meetings, and they'll be upset if we don't have them."*

> *"This report seems like a total waste of time, but I guess the other department is tracking all the data. I don't want to let anyone down."*

> *"I'm sure I should delegate this project, but it's a nice change of pace to work on something that's easy and sort of mindless. Besides, it would just take longer to explain it to someone else."*

It's almost impressive to hear leaders come up with so many reasons for marching on without reconsidering the value of a certain task or approach. Granted, sometimes leaders aren't given a choice in the matter. But when they do have options, they often don't take them.

One by one, these potentially limiting approaches chip away at a leader's ability to perform at an optimal level.

Solutions to
BREAK FREE

Today's forward-thinking leaders have realized that everything consuming their time must earn the right to be on their to-do list. To establish that competition, they have adopted a new approach.

Modern leaders deliberately take everything off auto-pilot.

And I do mean everything: Their perspectives. Their approaches. Their meetings. Their habits. Their initiatives. Their mindsets. Their tasks. Moving forward, every unconscious thought process and repetitive action become intentional rather than mindless. Conscious rather than automatic.

Modern leaders question all of it.

These leaders dig in to determine what's necessary – and what's not. Thoroughly. Objectively. Sacred cows included.

They ask themselves tough questions. Does this project or initiative still help to achieve the broader goals, no matter how big it is or how long it's been around? Is personal attachment clouding their professional judgment? I'm quite sure those uncomfortable questions were addressed at Nabob before the company cut two profitable brands with significant market share.

These leaders bravely put their precious to-do lists under the microscope. Which tasks and meetings are fueling the team's ability to meet and exceed goals? Which ones aren't? Are they engaging in behaviors that seem more like a product of muscle memory rather than choice? Could any of those tasks or actions be updated, upgraded, or even eliminated? Is there a better way?

Modern leaders determine what really matters.

We only have 24 hours in a day. It's not possible to negotiate for more, so we have to become more strategic about how we fill that time.

After answering some pointed questions, forward-thinking leaders have exactly what they need to conduct a systematic, cost/benefit analysis on everything that occupies their time and attention – their business functions, projects, habits, and tasks. It basically becomes a competition.

Everything they do has to prove its worth and earn the right to be there. If it doesn't add value or help move the team toward the goal, it's in jeopardy.

There's an interesting parallel here to the best-selling book from Marie Kondo called *The Life-Changing Magic of Tidying Up*. A highly respected Japanese organizing consultant, Kondo rose to global fame with her unique approach to decluttering physical spaces. While most organization experts focus on what to throw away, Kondo flips the script and emphasizes *what to keep.*

> *When people get real clarity about what's actually necessary and adds true value, it's much easier to let everything else go.*

This concept of "questioning everything and only keeping what matters" is beneficial for clutter-weary homeowners and busy leaders who are buried under the weight of their schedules. Interestingly, we can also see the impact of this thinking at the organizational level.

Executives at pharmaceutical giant Pfizer were facing a financial crisis in 2005. They realized budget-slashing alone wasn't going to solve their problems, so they got serious about finding ways to make their management team more efficient.

After research showed that leaders there were spending an inordinate amount of time during the workday on administrative or non-core tasks, the company introduced an innovative program called pfizerWorks.

With the click of an icon on their computers, leaders at Pfizer could instantly outsource low-value tasks to affordable, global resources. They could keep the tasks that really mattered while off-loading things such as scheduling meetings, creating spreadsheets, developing slides for presentations, doing research, or entering data for reports. The results were dramatic.

By eliminating the distractions and interruptions that had been crowding their schedules, these highly paid leaders could stay laser-focused on high-value tasks that made the company much more competitive. The organization now offers this productivity-boosting service to more than 10,000 of its managers, and the financial benefits speak for themselves.

Modern leaders make the commitment to let go.

This is the tough part. It's one thing to decide which actions and perspectives are most important, but letting go of everything else might be the biggest challenge.

Why? Even when leaders feel trapped by an endless treadmill of meetings and tedious paperwork, that level of chaos may have become *normal* for them. Even strangely comfortable. In fact, NOT doing all of those things would somehow feel wrong.

That same reluctance to let go occurs with business initiatives, too. Leaders may automatically push back if they are expected to abandon a popular project, close out a mature brand, or switch to a completely different IT system. After promoting a primary revenue driver for 12 months, it can feel disconcerting to shift gears and move on to something new.

The point here?

> *The success of letting go isn't just about minor, inconsequential things. It could involve giving up major, mission-critical business functions. And leaders find that incredibly difficult.*

It's an emotion captured by American author William Faulkner (and, later, echoed by novelist Stephen King): *"In writing, you must kill all your darlings."*

I'll explain.

Sometimes writers get very attached to certain phrases, sentences, or even full chapters. From an artistic standpoint, they just love the way the words are woven together or the mental images jump to life or the emotions feel painfully real. They take great pride in the stroke of creative genius that gave birth to those words and — like any parent — they lose all objectivity in judging them.

The thought of deleting those precious "darlings" seems unthinkable to the writer. Even when the editor points out that the words don't add anything to the story or move the plot along appropriately. It feels like a terrible dilemma, but Faulkner pointed out the cold, hard truth: If writers want to be successful, they have to be willing to sacrifice those "darlings" for the good of the reader. If the words don't serve a purpose, they have to go.

Today's most successful leaders and companies apply that same approach to their daily tasks, leadership habits, and business pursuits. They, of course, understand that their "darlings" exist in a different form, but they've learned to follow Faulkner's advice.

If it doesn't add value, they don't do it. They let it go. Really, really let it go.

One of the most stunning examples of this head-turning strategy comes from the leaders at Ford Motor Company. The iconic automotive manufacturer shocked consumers in 2018 with an announcement that seemed unimaginable. Over the next few years, Ford said it would streamline its product line in North America and — gasp! — stop making cars. Talk about killing your darlings! That's serious commitment.

Technically, the company plans to continue manufacturing the perennially popular Mustang and one crossover SUV, but the leaders have wholeheartedly committed to focus on the product lines with the greatest potential for success. They analyzed extensive financial data and, basically, made all of their vehicles compete to earn their way onto Ford's "To-Produce List." Trucks, utilities, and commercial vehicles made the cut; sedans did not.

We'd need a crystal ball to tell if that move is ultimately successful for Ford, but it's a brave strategy that seems to have merit and mirrors the trailblazing moves made by some of the most inventive executives of our time.

It takes rock-solid commitment for leaders to shed the old projects, tasks, and habits that are holding them down. There's a constant temptation to slide back into the old, familiar ways of doing and being. But for leaders and organizations alike, the dedication is worth it.

Strategies for
BREAKTHROUGH PERFORMANCE

If you recognize that it's time to do some pruning as part of your leadership strategy, here are a few specific ways you can get started:

Be clear on your goals.

What's your overriding purpose — for yourself, your team, and your organization? That's the most important guide for this entire exercise.

You need to know where you're going before you can find the best route to get there.

 ## 2 Use your goals as a filter for every potential project, task, or perspective.

These questions may be helpful as you prequalify your actions:

- *Does this move me or my team forward?*

- *Does this support department or company objectives?*

- *Does this further my growth and development?*

- *Am I doing this to drive results or to make someone else comfortable?*

- *Am I doing this because all of my colleagues/peers are doing it (and think I should do it, too)?*

- *If I stopped doing this, would anyone notice or care?*

- *If I stopped doing this, would it free me up to spend time on growing another part of the business or pursuing a more lucrative opportunity?*

- *Is this the best and highest use of my time and energy?*

Should you determine that a task or behavior does not contribute to reaching your goals, commit to letting it go. Make Faulkner proud, and kill your darlings.

Then take a strategic look at the high-value items remaining. Do you personally need to complete these tasks or could they be delegated (completely or in part)? Is there a smarter way to approach them so they create additional value? Even though they may have contributed to your success, consider whether a shift would allow you to get more involved in an area of greater interest.

Taking a fresh look at everything inevitably uncovers opportunities to improve efficiency.

Make a "Stop Doing" List.

If you're like most professionals, you've likely sharpened your rationalization skills over the years. Consider developing some tools that will help you stay on track with your new calendar of value-added-only entries.

Ironically, some leaders approach downsizing their to-do lists by... creating another list: a "Stop Doing List." (Unconventional thinking at its finest!) This is actually an excellent mental exercise and an important reminder of the new choices and habits that will guide your daily schedule.

Your "Stop Doing List" might include things such as:

- *I will stop saying "yes" to every request without first considering its worth.*

- *I will stop producing the monthly reports that no one is asking for.*

- *I will stop working every weekend.*

- *I will stop letting other people control my day and my time.*

- *I will stop allowing interruptions that hijack my schedule.*

- *I will stop attending meetings that don't pertain to my team's objectives.*

––––––––––––

Leaders today have strong incentives to demolish their dependence on what they've always done. Instead of resisting the counterintuitive prune-to-grow logic, they are embracing it. Narrowing their focus to expand their impact. Minimizing their actions to maximize performance. Doing less to achieve more.

Through the ingenuity of letting go, they are finding abundant success.

CHAPTER FIVE

"Refer to Chart B on page 431."

———————

DEFEAT
the Drag on
YOUR COMMUNICATION

A 46-year-old woman named Carina stood nervously in front of the members of the venture capital committee. She was asking them for an investment of $175,000 to help take her furniture business to the next level.

Carina had spent weeks preparing her pitch. She had PowerPoint slides and handouts. Economic indicators and statistics about trends for consumer spending in the home furnishings industry. She talked about the scalability of her business model, the opportunities to reduce costs for raw materials, and the anticipated ROI.

At the end of her extremely thorough presentation, she waited in silence for someone on the committee to respond.

A man at the end of the table took in a deep breath and slowly exhaled. Then he methodically removed his glasses, folded them, and set them on the table. He looked right at Carina and asked her the most important question – one that wasn't addressed in her slide deck.

"Can you explain why you are doing this?"

Answering that question wasn't exactly part of Carina's well-rehearsed speech, so it caught her a little off guard. After taking a moment to collect her thoughts, she began to share her story.

She was originally from Austria and had moved to America with her family when she was nine years old. It wasn't an easy transition. Her father made a living by building furniture using old-world techniques that had been passed down through several generations. Over time, happy customers spread the word about her dad's high-quality products – chairs, tables, desks, and hutches. Sales became relatively steady.

When Carina was old enough, she started working in the family business and also became a master craftsman. Since that time, she and her father teamed up to create and sell their unique furniture at a higher volume. Now, as product demand was dramatically escalating, her father's health was declining.

Carina knew she couldn't keep up with the orders on her own, but she recognized an opportunity to grow the business. To automate some of the processes. To hire a team of employees. To expand her market by selling online.

It would be a big leap for a small business, but Carina wanted to honor her father's sacrifice and keep her family's legacy alive.

As Carina described the true motivation behind her request for an investment, her passion and enthusiasm bubbled over. The emotionless stares of the committee members melted away to become warm smiles and nods.

In her excitement, Carina walked forward and handed the man an old, yellowed photograph. It showed her father and grandfather building a bench for the front porch of their small home in the Austrian countryside. That's where it all started.

This might not have been Carina's original approach for winning over potential investors, but it was the smartest thing she did.

She found success by authentically telling her story and using a photo to bring her message to life. That's how she connected with the people who sat in front of her.

Her research and projections were solid, but that's not what the committee members would remember weeks later. It was the story of a proud, hard-working entrepreneur and the picture of the ancestors who had inspired her. The impact was vastly different.

And yes, Carina got the cash infusion.

Leaders today face the same challenge when they communicate, whether they are trying to engage and motivate their teams, present a new strategy to the executive team, or interview for a higher-level position.

If they choose to go with the traditional approach of presenting audiences with an ocean of facts and statistics, their key messages will likely get swept away in the undertow.

Chains That
BIND US

When leaders don't update and clarify their communication goals, their messages may not make it through the clutter.

Leaders often communicate to inform, instruct, and impress.

Whether it starts in business schools, management training programs or on the job, leaders have been conditioned to communicate in what might be considered a relatively formal way. They become indoctrinated to the concept of what is (and isn't) appropriate for professional communication, and they follow that formula throughout their careers.

It becomes a practice. And they get plenty of reinforcement. According to the McKinsey Global Institute, leaders spend about 80% of their days communicating.

Unfortunately, leaders can get hopelessly sidetracked trying to inform, instruct, and even impress. They become so enthralled with transferring *information* that they lose sight of the need to transfer *meaning*.

Here's how they end up in that communication rut.

Familiar communication patterns tend to emerge among leaders who have become immersed in a particular industry or organization. They know they can accelerate the pace of conversations by working from a set of shared assumptions that are generally accepted by their colleagues and coworkers.

Along the way, they toss in acronyms, buzzwords, and key-project nicknames. Increase the SEO for B2B. Optimize the UX to increase EPS. Merge the Z-2A with the M-4B line from Q3. Again, that speeds up the discussion.

To make matters worse, leaders deliberately bolster their messages with a heavy dose of statistics, spreadsheets, and complex reports to help establish credibility. They want to look organized and proactive. Plus, there's a great chance all that factual information will stifle any potential objections. If it looks meticulously researched, people are more likely to buy in and move on without much thought, discussion, or challenges.

What started out as admirable approaches to communicate formally and professionally have turned into a cryptic, data-overloaded, jumbled mess. Sterile. Impersonal. And certainly not effective.

> *This formal, fact-heavy style of communicating no longer resonates with today's employees, particularly those in the younger generation.*

They want passion and transparency. They want to be engaged. To participate. Even co-create. No stuffy platitudes. No generic statements that fail to connect them to team objectives or invite them into the process.

If leaders can't mentally shift to communicate in a way that both informs *and* inspires, they will struggle to be seen as authentic, influential, and engaging.

Information overload can drown out a leader's messages.

Employes and leaders alike are bombarded with mountains of information every day, and it's virtually impossible to keep up with all of it.

An article in *Forbes* by scientific writer David DiSalvo puts this process in perspective. Through our senses, our brains gather roughly 11 million bits of information per second from the environment around us. However, our conscious minds only have the capacity to process about 40 of those at once.

It reminds me of the all-too-common reference about trying to drink from a fire hose.

From the moment we wake up, we face the daunting task of sorting through the barrage of information that invades our minds.

Television, radio, emails, text messages, websites, social media, pod-casts, billboards. Add in face-to-face conversations, webinars, phone calls, and group meetings. And then "helpful leaders" crank up into hyper-communication mode to share anything and everything.

The outrageously cluttered information landscape is mind-boggling. With so many things competing for our attention during the workday, we can't possibly take it all in. We have to pick and choose. We filter some things out. We ignore others completely. And we don't always make the right choices.

In fact, there's a fair chance we will misinterpret at least some of the communications we receive during the day. The *Training Magazine* 2014 Industry Report quantified the financial cost of that problem.

According to their studies, a business with 100 employees spends an average downtime of 17 hours per week clarifying communications that weren't correctly understood. That translates to a cost of more than $525,000 per year. For bigger companies, the number goes up.

Information overload comes with a steep price tag (literally!), and leaders tend to forget the enormous amount of competition they face when trying to communicate with their teams. The backdrop of noise is loud and intense.

Solutions to
BREAK FREE

Successful leaders have discovered some innovative ways to over-come these challenges and deliver their messages more effectively and authentically.

Modern leaders communicate to engage, inspire, and influence.

Today's pioneering leaders understand the difficulties of communicating in our chaotic climate, but they have learned to think about the process in a new way. They know that success isn't measured by the information transferred; it's based on the *experience created*.

I must admit this is an area where I have to remain vigilant. In my work as a keynote speaker, I am all about added value. I have a natural tendency to pack as much information as possible into my allotted time with an audience. Business insights. Scientific findings. Meaty takeaways.

On one hand, it makes sense to be sure people get their money's worth. On the other hand, my efforts to over-prepare could easily become overwhelming. Or worse yet, not engaging.

I have to regularly remind myself that the *experience* is just as important as the *content*. What will my presentation really mean for the audience? What will they remember? How can I bring my message to life?

That's the secret.

> *It's not about the information. It's not about the quantity of facts shared. It's about the experience we provide.*

Modern leaders embrace this novel idea of disrupting their typical approach to communication. They start in reverse. Instead of trying to determine what information needs to go out, they concentrate on the end result. What impact do they want to make? What are the challenges and perspectives of their audience members? What experience would they like to create?

With that in mind, they focus on the message instead of the data. They peel away all the layers of complexity that have been clogging up their communication and get down to messages that are authentic and engaging. They present them in novel ways. And they aren't afraid to open a window into their motives and rationale.

They refuse to let themselves take the easy way out when they communicate with their teams. Yes, it's tempting to pull up the existing charts for last quarter's performance and simply update them with the new numbers before sending them out. But they realize the old, tired charts aren't cutting it. No one is paying attention.

If they really want to engage their teams to refocus, they have to switch things up. Find alternative approaches. Get creative. Perhaps incorporate imaginative props. Become the architect of an experience that cuts through all the noise.

These modern leaders also understand the importance of communicating to inspire their teams and help them envision the future. And when they make that a priority, employees can do a better job of bridging the gap between current products and those that consumers don't even know they will be demanding.

When leaders make a choice to strive for this broader, deeper, and more compelling brand of communication that genuinely resonates, they can deliver meaning – and make meaningful connections along the way.

Modern leaders use stories to bring information to life.

An article in *Psychology Today* described a unique experiment that used MRIs to monitor human brain activity as people consumed different types of information. Certain parts of the participants' brains would "light up" when they read a newspaper article. Other parts were activated when they looked at a painting or heard someone reading a technical document.

But when the facilitator started to tell a story, brain activity increased in multiple areas — auditory, visual, sensory, reasoning, emotions. The findings proved that we use much more of our brains when we are listening to a story. Additional studies showed that we are 6-7 times more likely to remember information if it is presented in story form.

That's an important secret weapon for leaders who want to create a better experience and communicate with more meaningful messages. Stories draw us in like nothing else.

When Herb Kelleher founded Southwest Airlines, he had a vision that storytelling would be a continuous part of the corporate fabric. He knew his employees needed access to a steady stream of operating information every day to be effective in their jobs, but he also wanted to consistently tell the stories that defined the organization's bigger purpose.

Still today, team members from HR regularly travel with a camera crew in search of Southwest employees who have become heroes in the personal stories of their passengers. They create heart-tugging videos that feature actual customer stories and the poignant tales of people facing real-life struggles. In each true story, a Southwest employee steps in to save the day.

One video featured an interview with a female passenger who had been training for months to compete in a strenuous, 12-person Ragnar Relay in the Cumberland Mountains. Her flight arrived safely the afternoon before the Relay, but the suitcase with her race gear and shoes did not. She left the airport in a total panic. During the night, a Southwest gate agent tracked down her bag and drove it three hours (one way) to make sure the passenger had everything she needed before the race began.

Besides celebrating their exceptional customer service, these moving videos demonstrate the actual power of sharing stories. They have proven to be extremely successful tools for influencing other Southwest employees and inspiring them to become heroes for their own passengers. Even more impressive, the power of storytelling shows up in the bottom line.

In 2018, J.D. Power once again ranked Southwest Airlines as the highest in customer satisfaction among low-cost carriers in North America.

Another example comes from Airbnb, the online hospitality marketplace.

In November 2016, Airbnb's CEO Brian Chesky unveiled a new app called Trips at the company's Open Conference. He stood on the stage at the historic Orpheum Theater in downtown Los Angeles in front of a huge audience.

Rather than kicking off the presentation with a discussion about the slick technical functionality of the new app, he showed a picture from one of his family vacations as a child. He then shared a few stories from some other past trips that shaped the person he had become.

As a master storyteller, Chesky found a clever way to demonstrate the value of Airbnb's new offering. With the app, customers can do more than find lodging in different locations. They can log on and select unique experiences at these destinations that will transform their trips into unforgettable memories.

They could book surfing lessons in Hawaii with an expert from the World Surf League. Spend a day herding sheep with a local family in Ireland. Or take a bike tour through orchards in Bangkok on the way to a Thai cooking class.

After Chesky used his own experiences to set the stage for this new app, the audience was fully on board. They intrinsically understood the value of the offering, and they were eager to do their part to see it transform the market.

Modern leaders have learned the wisdom and value of telling stories. It's a brilliant way to capture imagination and invite their audiences to join them on a mental journey.

Modern leaders are strategic with message format, delivery, and visuals.

FORMAT

Successful leaders take the time to craft messages that are simple, concise, and compelling. Understandably, that requires more effort, but it's essential if they want to communicate in a way that is clutter-busting, brain-activating, and impact-making.

> *There's a real art to condensing the essence of a*
> *message's meaning into a very small package.*

English business magnate Richard Branson once said, *"If your idea can't fit on the back of an envelope, it's rubbish."* He makes a great point.

DELIVERY

Being able to deliver those concise messages in a powerful and authentic way is also a strong differentiator. To help future leaders hone that skill, the University of Virginia's Darden School of Business has adopted a new approach. The faculty doesn't just expect its students to take public speaking courses. They put them in front of a crowd to try stand-up comedy and improvisation.

By learning the techniques typically found in top acting classes — speaking, listening, reading the crowd, and thinking quickly on their feet — these students learn how to enhance their delivery of communication and to be fully present with their audiences. Those skills will become priceless during corporate meetings and boardroom negotiations.

VISUALS

The other side of the message-delivery coin involves the importance of using visuals. According to research done by 3M, visual communication can inform up to 60,000 times faster than words. Don't tell me; show me.

On social media, posts accompanied by images are reportedly 10 times more likely to receive engagement. And if those visuals are in color? The willingness to read the post goes up by 80%.

> *Visuals aren't just great for attracting attention; they also get results.*

In a study from the *Educational Technology Research and Development Journal,* researchers compared the ability of people to follow instructions that included text with an illustration versus those who received text only. The visual support improved the success of completing the task by a whopping 323%.

And how about messages intended to influence decisions or change attitudes? Visuals can help to seal the deal. A study conducted at the Wharton School of Business at the University of Pennsylvania found that 50% of a typical audience will be persuaded by a message that is presented verbally, while 67% will be persuaded when verbal messages are reinforced with accompanying visuals.

Successful leaders can gain a distinct advantage by strategically designing their communication. They create laser-focused messages destined for high impact. They cleverly bring them to life with smart imagery. And they deliver them with poise, professionalism, and an undeniable presence.

Strategies for
BREAKTHROUGH PERFORMANCE

To break out of old communication patterns that no longer provide value, follow these steps to update your approach:

Focus on the experience.

Move past the idea of just informing your team or your audience. Instead, expand to have a broader communication goal that involves engaging and influencing. Keep in mind that you aren't just transferring facts; you want to provide an experience.

To make that kind of connection, think about the messages you want to share in terms of your audience's perspective. The information you deliver needs to be meaningful from their viewpoint.

- *What's the one thing you want them to understand and remember, above all else?*

- *What do you want them to think or feel as a result of your communication?*

- *What change or action would you like to prompt?*

- *What experience do you want to create?*

The other critical aspect of providing an experience is determining which message-delivery format will allow you to make the biggest impact. Maybe that's in-person or online. It could mean communicating individually or in a group.

Take time to consider the different options.

- *Are there ways to make your message more of an interactive dialogue and less of a brain dump?*

- *Could you add humor or levity to help diffuse an otherwise-stressful situation?*

- *How can you support your message with striking visuals?*

- *Is your message worthy of being translated into some form of media presentation?*

- *Would someone else do a better job sharing this information?*

- *Could you parcel out the data to multiple presenters and combine efforts?*

2 Make it easy for people to extract your main message.

Help your audience separate the wheat from the chaff by narrowing the scope of your communication to highlight the key elements.

- *Drill down to feature the most relevant factors in your message and explain exactly why they matter*

- *Provide context for your message in a way that builds rapport and gives the audience a reason to connect with the bigger meaning*

- *Commit to reducing information overload rather than adding to the clutter*

3 Share powerful stories.

Give your messages a knock-out punch by weaving them into a narrative form that truly resonates with your audience.

- *Incorporate stories and anecdotes to provide memorable context for your communications*

- *Use metaphors and analogies to illustrate your key points*

- *Consider props to draw the audience in from a different angle*

- *Fold in rich imagery that engages different parts of the brain*

- *Tap into emotions so that the audience feels a stronger connection to the subject*

- *Support your stories with video, still images, or music*

- *Hold attention by including a surprise or twist they didn't see coming*

Storytelling doesn't always come naturally for some leaders. If you're one of them, explore the many courses (on- and off-line) that can help you increase these skills.

———————

Leaders who can destroy the drag on their communication can significantly expand their professional influence. By crawling out of their communication ruts and strengthening their connections to their audiences, they can deliver meaningful messages that create positive experiences and leave lasting impressions.

CHAPTER SIX

"Trust me. I know this stuff inside and out."

BREAK FREE
from the
EXPERT TRAP

Students of the martial arts begin their journeys wearing white belts that indicate they are beginners in the practice. As they work through the training and demonstrate their skills, they can advance to higher levels as indicated by a series of colored belts – yellow, orange, green, blue, purple, brown, and red. Only then, after a period of months, years or even decades, the most dedicated students reach the pinnacle of success: the honor of wearing the coveted black belts.

Becoming a black belt in martial arts is widely recognized as a significant achievement. We've all seen movies and television programs that feature characters who are portrayed as black belts in sports such as Karate, Judo, or Jiujitsu. With one subtle wardrobe choice, the directors can communicate to the audience that these martial arts experts are at the very top of their game in strategic self-defense. They are perceived to be masters of their craft.

Here's what many people don't know.
The black belt isn't the final step in
the process. Not by a long shot.

The black color actually represents a belt that is "soiled" with experience and signifies the endless capacity for additional knowledge. In that respect, earning the distinction of the black belt is simply a point along an ongoing, boundless journey. A place where expertise reunites with new beginnings.

According to the World Martial Arts Center, earning the coveted black belt is "a never-ending process of self-growth, knowledge, and enlightenment."

Those who earn the black belts may become teachers and mentors, but they also cross-train with other martial arts students of every level to share experiences. They firmly believe that wisdom and insights may come from unlikely sources – even novices in the sport.

The point is, these black-belt experts maintain a gracious, welcoming attitude with a sincere willingness to learn wherever and from whomever they can. They have the discipline to set aside their vast accomplishments and toss out the mental baggage that comes with it. No reliance on usual patterns or old habits. They look at new challenges with a beginner's eyes.

Every option is worthy of consideration, despite knowing what worked in the past. Essentially, they remove their experience bias and allow their minds to become a clean slate. Open to more innovative solutions. Ready for deeper learning.

The underlying message from this example deserves serious consideration by those in the corporate world.

Leaders (like martial arts students) have traditionally been willing to put in the time and effort to advance their craft. These goal-oriented professionals are often sprinting toward a very defined finish line in a race that will position them as the masters in their fields – experts in management or a particular subject-matter area.

What they don't know is that this frantic race to the professional version of black-belt status is not the end of the journey. If they refuse to acknowledge that the ladder has more rungs, they may face some unanticipated hurdles.

Chains That
BIND US

Leaders who become overly attached to their own expertise may begin to suffer from negative consequences.

Experts may run the risk of career atrophy.

For years, professionals have purposely sought out expert status to set themselves apart and add value for their organizations. They work hard to build credibility and become their teams' go-to resources. The thought leaders. The people with the deepest knowledge in a particular slice of the industry. Their path to career success involved amassing more expertise in a niche category than anyone else.

Instead of looking at the color of their belts to find evidence of their progress, we can look at their impressive resumes. They typically have a mile-long list of advanced certifications or even fancy degrees. Perhaps the thought leaders have written influential white papers, contributed to their industry journals, or received patents for their groundbreaking work. These credentials cumulatively tighten their careers and become their "claims to fame."

> *While companies certainly rely on employees with expertise, it's important to note that this classic approach to knowledge acquisition can also become a barrier for career advancement.*

Today, the intrinsic nature of business is fluctuating at a dizzying pace. Leaders who aren't constantly on a mission to seek out a broad array of perspectives may run the risk of becoming outdated and irrelevant. While their colleagues are displaying the agility to cross over different roles and functions to support the organization's changing needs, these experts may become pigeonholed. And their careers could become stuck.

Experts may inadvertently become more closed-minded.

A Japanese monk named Shunryu Suzuki succinctly described this phenomenon:

> "In the beginner's mind, there are many possibilities. In the expert's mind, there are few."

The truth of that statement can be backed up by solid research.

A scientist named Victor Ottati at Loyola University conducted a series of experiments to analyze behavior changes based on the different roles people play. He wanted to know whether individuals embody the characteristics associated with a particular role when they are in that position.

For instance, if you happen to see your family doctor in the local department store, her demeanor and actions will probably be different than what you would experience sitting in her office as a patient. The context of the interaction changes the attitudes and behaviors. Ottati wanted to know how that translated to the role of an expert.

This wasn't an easy thing to measure, since true subject matter experts have valid reasons to interact with authority and confidence. Ottati worked around that by removing the actual expertise from the equation and only looking at the impact of *perceived* expertise.

He and his team brought in some volunteers of roughly equal intelligence to take an IQ-type assessment and complete a group task. While they believed they were all taking the same test, some of the people were given a very difficult version and others received a highly simplistic one.

Before the volunteers were asked to participate in an exercise together, they were provided with their test results. As you might guess, one-half received extremely high scores, and the other half, extremely low.

The behavior shifts during the exercise that followed were quite interesting.

The low-scoring individuals were more open to new ideas and collaborating with their teammates. Those who scored higher (the "artificially smart" volunteers) seemed to internalize their relative success on the test. They were less likely to listen to other opinions, and they were more likely to trust their own answers. In short, they automatically assumed their personal approaches were correct.

The experiment clearly showed that the participants who considered themselves to be experts with superior intelligence were more closed-minded than those who just experienced a failure on the test. Ottati calls this the *earned dogmatism effect*.

The same thing can happen to leaders.

They may subconsciously believe that their ideas have greater value because of their credentials and track record.

In some cases, they may be right. They probably rose through the organization for good reasons.

However, this type of skewed thinking can also make them more closed-minded and even immune to innovative concepts. Allowing that attitude to cloud their judgment comes with a huge risk of potentially missing the next big breakthrough or strategy for success that emanates from someone perceived to be less qualified.

Solutions to
BREAK FREE

French Novelist Marcel Proust once said, *"The real voyage of discovery consists not in finding new lands but in seeing with new eyes."*

He hit the nail on the head.

Modern leaders who are forging a new path toward success are committed to metaphorically resigning their roles as experts and approaching tasks with the spirit of a beginner.

Just like the black belts in martial arts think of their journeys as a never-ending road, these leaders are opening the door to broad, continuous learning – without any mental constraints about where or how that might happen.

How do they accomplish that?

Modern leaders regularly put themselves in positions to learn and grow.

Successful leaders and experts break away from the habit of earned dogmatism, and they try to approach new challenges with the mind-set of a novice rather than a know-it-all.

When HR guru Laszlo Bock was serving as Google's Senior VP of People Operations, he was interviewed about what he really looked for in new hires. His answer, perhaps shockingly, had nothing to do with high-tech experience. He wanted employees with *humility*.

Sounds strange on the surface, but Bock firmly believes that humble people are the key to greater success for organizations. Why? They never feel "finished" with the search for knowledge and have a genuine desire to learn from others at any level. That humility creates the space for others to contribute and, according to Bock, is a proven indicator for productive collaboration and innovative thinking.

> *Today's leaders need to deliberately put themselves in positions to humbly learn and grow. Every single day.*

To be honest, that's a difficult task. Accomplished professionals are usually very comfortable doing whatever they have always done to get positive results. They've got a system. They capture the efficiencies of repeated processes. They've built a reputation on it.

Continuously swimming into unknown waters can be unsettling, but modern leaders do it anyway. Growth and learning become an essential priority. This could mean challenging themselves by taking classes in a radically different area or immersing themselves in the client experience like they've never done before.

These savvy leaders amplify their performance by approaching challenges with the eyes of a novice and a healthy dose of humility.

Modern leaders have the confidence to admit they don't know everything.

In most organizations, there's an underlying expectation that leaders and experts have all the answers. Or they know right where to find them. The concept of not knowing might seem…well, awkward. Team members come to rely on that constant source of knowledge, and it can be disconcerting for them to discover that it's all a mirage.

The fact is, leaders don't know everything. They aren't infallible. They don't have all the answers. And it takes an enormous level of confidence to break out of the infinitely-wise-expert mold and openly admit that.

Oddly enough, some leaders are finding that the vulnerability involved in saying "I don't know" is energizing their teams in surprising ways.

Junior-level employees suddenly can't become complacent, expecting every answer to be provided to them by the powers above. When they aren't handed a clear solution, fact-finding becomes just as much their responsibility. They are required to flex their own critical-thinking muscles on a regular basis and work to solve problems in their own unique ways.

Through this process of shared discovery, the entire team shifts into a more active gear and focuses on group contributions to winning solutions. And that can have a significant impact on the bottom line.

Modern leaders value the questions as much as the answers.

As the story goes, Albert Einstein was once asked what he would do if he had one hour to solve a problem and his life depended on it. His response? He'd spend the first 55 minutes determining the proper question to ask.

He really was a genius.

Successful leaders today have learned to value questions just as much as the answers. And, perhaps more importantly, they work hard to ask the right questions — many of which start with, *"What if...?"*

What if we approach this challenge from the opposite direction? What if we tried using a different distribution model to expand our market share? What if we ignore our competitor's latest price cut and just find a way to add more value? What am I missing here?

> *These business trailblazers are bypassing their own know-how in favor of asking tough questions that could unearth something better, faster, or stronger.*

They refuse to be lulled into a false sense of security by their expert titles. They open up conversations for lively debate. They allow their insatiable curiosity to bubble up and inspire their teams to search for new products, services, or processes that better meet customer needs. Or reduce costs in unusual ways. Or generate more revenue.

Modern leaders accept the idea that mistakes can pay off.

In the past, leaders tried to do everything in their power to avoid making errors. They guarded their decisions and budgets and initiatives with a fierce, don't-rock-the-boat attitude.

Today, some leaders are throwing that rigidity right out the window. Instead of avoiding failure, they pursue it. Modern leaders are openly encouraging their teams to make mistakes, take greater risks, and be perfectly fine with failure.

In 2017, the new CEO of Coca-Cola Co., James Quincey, called for the organization's managers to let go of the fear of failure that was slowing them down.

Remember "New Coke"? None of the leaders wanted to be responsible for another misstep of that proportion, so they were playing it safe. Quincey pushed back, saying: *"If we're not making mistakes, we're not trying hard enough."*

That sentiment is also captured by the leaders at Grey Advertising, an iconic, New York-based agency with scores of award-winning campaigns. Their entire business is based on the ability of employees to think creatively without being limited by the fear of failure. Some ideas work; some don't. But the biggest duds often lead to the greatest opportunities for learning.

With that in mind, Grey's leaders established the "Heroic Failure Award." This honor celebrates someone who bravely pushed the boundaries of creativity, even though the idea ended in an epic fail. No judgment. No penalty. The winner holds on to the coveted trophy until the next gargantuan failure occurs. The trophy moves on, but winners keep the team's admiration for off-the-charts risk-taking.

Forward-thinking leaders relish this upside-down perspective. They know that experts have likely failed more times than beginners have tried.

> *Success is often built on the aftermath of failure, and the mistakes actually help to create the rich textures of their wisdom.*

Modern leaders are deliberate about courageously replacing safe approaches with ones that are emboldened and aggressive. They understand they can't win every bet. But, as the saying goes, they'll miss every shot they don't take.

With that said, these leaders aren't making foolish or uncalculated moves. They find strategic ways to limit their exposure by using test markets, soft rollouts, or short-term trials. But along the way, they prove over and over again that they aren't afraid to GO FOR IT.

If an idea totally bombs, leaders can learn from the experience and use that knowledge on the next big risk. If an experiment comes with a failure rate of 70%, leaders would be wise to push their employees to *fail faster*. The sooner they learn what doesn't work, the sooner they'll discover what does.

That's remarkably counterintuitive *and* positively brilliant.

Strategies for
BREAKTHROUGH PERFORMANCE

To help you resign your role as an expert and expand your influence, try following these strategic steps:

 Reframe the way you think about failure.

Every failure is another step along the road toward success. It's all part of the learning process.

Some of the world's greatest innovations emerged after enormous failures, and those errors actually paved the way for something much bigger and better. Remind yourself to think about risk-taking as experiments and opportunities rather than terrifying, white-knuckle moves with the potential for disaster.

It's OK to take risks. No, scratch that. It's *necessary* to take risks. If you want to establish a continuous pattern of success, you have to give yourself permission to fail. Be smart about it, but never let fear prevent you from going for it. Failure is part of the journey.

 Broaden the scope of your knowledge.

To compete in today's environment, you've got to be willing to kiss your comfort zone goodbye.

Actively work to balance your depth of knowledge in a certain area with a breadth of new experiences. If you've always worn the expert hat, think about ways to make yourself more valuable as a generalist.

By shifting your concentration from "what you know" to "what you don't know," you can transform the way you contribute to the organization in more formidable times. And, in many cases, you can avoid being pigeonholed as someone who isn't in tune with the bigger picture.

Make the commitment to pursue specialized development outside your normal scope of expertise and stretch your mind in unexpected ways.

- *Select projects that move you closer to your organization's core strategy*

- *Apply for a regional, national, or global role*

- *Take advantage of high-potential or rotation-group programs where participants are routinely exposed to complex business simulations*

- *Volunteer to take on a project that no one else wants*

- *Attend classes or seminars (in person/online) to learn about trending topics such as design thinking, mindfulness, change management, predictive analysis, or artificial intelligence*

Adopt the practice of constantly asking good questions.

Resist the temptation to over-rely on your own expertise, and let go of the need to always have the right answers.

This requires suspending your natural inclination to solve problems based on what you already know and what you've done in the past. Slow down. Don't form instant opinions or jump to conclusions. Be intentional about tapping into your well of curiosity and ask the questions that can uncover greater insights or alternative directions.

- *What's the real problem here?*

- *What haven't we taken into account?*

- *What risks are involved?*

- *What happens if we do nothing at all?*

- *Is there a different perspective we aren't considering?*

- *Is this an opportunity in disguise?*

- *What if we try something completely different?*

This strategy also comes into play when you are coaching and mentoring your team members. They may approach you as the expert with hopes of receiving a meaty knowledge download that will help to accelerate their careers. But the best thing you can do for them is to resist that urge. Focus on asking them some insight-provoking questions – ones that will prompt deeper thinking and help them develop an enviable skill for decisive problem-solving.

- *How do you see the situation?*

- *Why does this matter in light of the organization/team goals?*

- *What have you done so far?*

- *What's the biggest challenge for you?*

- *What risks and opportunities are involved?*

- *What are your plans for moving forward?*

- *What do you need to stop doing to reach your goal?*

Accomplished leaders are accelerating their careers by breaking free from the expert trap. They no longer allow themselves to remain captives of their expertise. They are finding the courage to change the tired, old narrative with a new attitude, some genuine vulnerability, the never-ending desire to learn, and a list of killer questions that can catapult their teams toward unprecedented success.

CHAPTER SEVEN

"Let's benchmark our competitors."

CAST OFF
the Blind Commitment
TO BEST PRACTICES

Picture the traditional bank lobby. Customers are waiting in line to open new accounts, make deposits, or withdraw funds. Each person slowly weaves forward on the path defined by the rope barriers and eventually approaches one of the tellers positioned behind a long counter.

Since customers make frequent trips to the bank, the tellers often greet them by name and personally help them with all their banking needs.

Enter the era of tech-savvy, smartphone-wielding customers.

Leaders in the banking industry quickly realized that the old business model wasn't going to fly with this newest crop of consumers. In response, they strategically developed infrastructures that would allow people to conduct their banking online *without ever stepping inside the bank lobby.* Convenience-craving customers loved it.

Suddenly, providing the ability to complete every financial transaction from the sofa in the middle of the night became a banking best practice. Instead of an option, it became a benchmark standard.

While Capital One Bank wholeheartedly met the challenges of the digital evolution, its leaders also made the strategic decision to defy the essence of this best practice. They believed the pendulum that started on one side with face-to-face banking had swung too far in the other direction, resulting in the near-commodity state of digital anonymity.

The leaders knew they still had to offer the full array of digital banking tools, but they also wanted to connect with their customers on a more personal level. To build relationships with them. To generate long-term loyalty.

That's when it happened.

Capital One Bank made the bold move to zig when everyone else was zagging.

At a time when many banks were reducing their offices because of slow traffic, Capital One Bank started opening new facilities — but definitely NOT your typical bank branches. The Starbucks-like retail locations, known as Capital One Cafes, began opening in selected cities to bridge the gap for consumers between the worlds of digital and personal.

These Cafes feature comfortable, inviting spaces with free Wi-Fi for public co-working, regardless of whether people are Capital One customers. They offer no-fee ATMs (again, available to everyone).

High-end coffee and beverages are available for purchase, as well as pastries made by local bakeries. Capital One "Ambassadors" are on hand to answer any banking questions, and patrons can also get free advice from Money Coaches in a casual, no-sales-pitch, no-pressure format.

Without a doubt, this was a stunning departure from the rest of the industry.

In the banking world, this strategy raised a few eyebrows. Some people were even quick to call it a foolish concept. But based on the bank's ambitious expansion plans, the company must be seeing positive results.

Will this rebel choice pay off long-term? Only time will tell. But the bank certainly found a creative way to meet its customers' needs while also building a unique sense of community.

A number of organizations like Capital One Bank have found success by moving beyond the constraints of best practices, but others can't seem to escape the cycle of following industry standards. To be fair, it's tough to swim upstream. I know from experience that benchmarking has an irresistible draw. But when leaders choose to go with the flow, they may lose out on potential opportunities that could enhance and redefine their careers.

Chains That
BIND US

If leaders allow themselves (and their teams) to mindlessly float along with the current of best practices, they are significantly limiting their options. Rather than making a move to break away from the pack, they are solidifying their "sameness." And that short-sighted view comes with big drawbacks.

We are conditioned to imitate successful strategies.

By definition, a best practice is a professional procedure that is widely accepted as being the most effective. It's considered to be the correct way to produce the optimal results. Companies spend large amounts of money on benchmarking to help them align their business practices and performance metrics with the accepted industry standards.

Perhaps there's a little irony there.

While it's considered cheating for a student to copy from someone else's paper, companies today encourage this kind of "copying."

From a business perspective, it's not as opportunistic as it sounds. Following best practices can be a great tool to help save time and money. We can observe what worked (or what didn't) among our competitors and colleagues, and we can use that knowledge to jumpstart our own success stories. We borrow. We adopt. We recycle.

In theory, imitation seems like a smart way to grab a piece of the pie without having to bake it. But many times, that just doesn't work.

Best practices go stale faster today.

We're naturally inclined to stick with whatever is already working. If we can follow best practices that someone else perfected, we can speed up our process, reduce the risk of failure, and increase the odds of success. It's hard to argue with that time-saving logic.

The problem is, best practices have a limited shelf life.

Leaders may become so consumed with benchmarking that they stop thinking about processes from an objective viewpoint. Instead, they just continue to rely on best-practice assumptions and mimic past performance. Like someone at the gym who's mindlessly walking on the treadmill. Step after step. Mile after mile. Without even thinking about it.

> *Many leaders today have allowed themselves to get into a trance-like state with benchmarking, and they don't notice when the results start to drop off.*

A few years ago, I had the opportunity to sit down with the Vice President of Marketing for North America at Dell Technologies, and he shared with me an interesting story about his first order of business upon accepting that position.

He sent out a request to everyone in his division and asked them to submit a list of any initiatives or best practices that once added value but had basically run their course. His goal was to determine up front which ones were no longer effective or producing adequate results.

A few weeks later, he asked his assistant to compile the full list for him to review. It ended up being a very short list, as only two people had responded.

He followed up by sending another request and ensured his new team members that their responses wouldn't be viewed as criticisms or negative attitudes. Their input was important to help him sweep away any potentially outdated thinking and replace it with new or different practices.

As he began having personal conversations with people about this assignment, he realized their hesitance wasn't related to the fear of being viewed as a complainer. These employees simply weren't used to viewing best practices as commodities that could wear out or become obsolete with overuse.

Once they fully understood his motivation, they took a more objective look at things. Suggestions poured in. And ultimately, he ended up with a solid list of best practices that were ripe for retooling or removing.

While best practices have always evolved over time, today they are going stale faster than ever. They are reaching the point of diminishing returns at an almost alarming rate. It can be blatantly unnerving to admit that what works well today may not work tomorrow.

If leaders don't actively and frequently push their teams to evaluate the effectiveness of an adopted best practice, people can end up drowning in initiatives and practices that are no longer meaningful for reaching critical goals.

Best practices aren't a one-size-fits-all solution.

What works brilliantly for one company doesn't always work for another one. When leaders try to "cut and paste" the industry best practices and apply them to their businesses, they may be in for a bumpy ride. Organizations are different. Employees are different. Customers are different.

One solution can't possibly be the answer for every company in the marketplace, so there are serious drawbacks to making generic standards the automatic default.

This disconnect is particularly evident when best practices are developed in one country and then applied on a global basis. What works in South Carolina probably won't work as well in South Korea. These approaches literally get lost in translation.

When it comes to best practices, leaders tend to forget that industry standards don't always make the leap to other companies OR other cultures. And when that happens, they are limiting the ability of their teams to perform at the highest level.

Solutions to
BREAK FREE

Today's most successful leaders appreciate the intrinsic value of best practices, but they don't consider them to be hard-and-fast rules that MUST be followed. They approach them with a respectful grain of salt.

Modern leaders are comfortable playing the role of rebel.

For these progressive leaders, it's not just about a willingness to *bend* the rules. They set out to be envelope-pushing pioneers. They refuse to plagiarize another company's success story, word for word.

Instead, when it makes sense, they make a statement by openly defying best practices. They snap out of the trance and pursue the vast potential hiding within the discovery of divergent approaches.

One of the best examples of this type of defiance occurred in the movie industry.

The first Blockbuster Video opened in October 1985 in Dallas, Texas. Having a retail presence allowed producers to continue earning revenue on their movies even after their big-screen showings came to an end. For the general public, these video stores provided an exciting, new way to consume entertainment.

The business model wasn't without its flaws. Customers were willing to drive to their local video rental stores to pick up their favorite rom-coms or action flicks, but they really, really hated driving back to return them by the due date. So they procrastinated. The late fees often piled up. And inevitably, the videotapes (and later, DVDs) prompted intense family negotiations. *("Please! I'll do all the laundry if you'll go return the movies before we get charged for another day.")*

Despite the minor issues, these retail stores were highly successful. As competitors popped up, they followed best practices but tried to differentiate themselves by offering lower pricing, newer movies, or longer rental periods.

As legend has it, a businessman named Reed Hastings had to pay $40 for returning a rental movie past the deadline and decided to funnel his frustration into a new business opportunity. He partnered with colleague Marc Randolph to closely analyze the policies and procedures followed by video rental stores. Together, they came to a firm conclusion: The industry best practices needed a radical overhaul.

That's how Netflix was born.

Co-founders Hastings and Randolph flipped the whole business model upside down. No retail stores. No late charges. And customers could order as many movies to watch at home as they wanted for a small, monthly subscription fee.

Industry analysts were highly skeptical. In the early days, Netflix customers would receive and return their movies in padded envelopes through the U.S. Postal Service. That required customers to plan ahead for what they wanted to watch and then wait a few days for the movies to arrive. Not a perfect system, but still relatively popular.

Once the technology to enable video streaming was developed, Netflix was perfectly positioned to deliver instant entertainment with maximum convenience. Customers were already accustomed to paying those monthly subscription fees, and the value they received went way, way up.

> *It's safe to say that going in a completely different direction was an audaciously, game-changing strategy for Netflix.*

As of July 2018, Netflix had more than 125 million streaming subscribers worldwide, and 64.5% of digital video viewers in the U.S. watched Netflix at least once every month.

Modern leaders take pride in being benchmark-breakers.

Another example of this behavior comes from the vacuum cleaner industry.

For more than 80 years, consumers who purchased vacuum cleaners were essentially entering into a long-term relationship with the manufacturer. A major part of the companies' revenue streams came from replacement bags that customers had to buy regularly to continue using the product. That was the business model, and that's how the industry worked.

When industrial design engineer James Dyson invented the first bagless vacuum, no manufacturer wanted to produce his model. He was rejected by everyone in the business. Hard pass. They believed that eliminating vacuum bags was a ludicrous idea that would eat away at their profits and eventually drive them all out of business.

Dyson was still not willing to follow those rules. He eventually set up his own manufacturing company and, within two years, he was producing the best-selling vacuum cleaners in Britain. As of 2017, the Dyson company was bringing in approximately $3 billion annually from its "outrageous" bagless vacuums and a variety of other imaginative products.

Today's rule-breaking leaders have the courage and confidence to promote innovative solutions that move in reverse from their competitors.

Initially, that may seem counterintuitive. Maybe even crazy. But they refuse to settle for working from the same blueprint as everyone else, even when it involves risk and ridicule.

Success for these leaders means having the guts to defy best practices and create their own. And when they do, the rewards can be significant.

Strategies for
BREAKTHROUGH PERFORMANCE

To resist being shackled by the constraints of benchmarking, try following these steps for inspiration:

 Be strategic about applying your industry's standards.

Best practices still have value and are worthy of consideration. The key to success is analyzing them — strategically and proactively — rather than simply accepting them. It's critical to determine which standards make sense for your company to emulate and which ones could be holding you back.

To help make that decision, ask yourself these questions:

- *Why are companies following this standard?*

- *When did this practice first start?*

- *What are the benefits and risks of following this best practice?*

- *Does it really apply to our organization/customers?*

- *Do you understand the impact of any new compliance regulations?*

- *What applies in the U.S. but not on a global basis?*

- *Are there trends on the horizon now that will soon make current best practices obsolete?*

- *How can we anticipate those changes and find a better way?*

 ## Question your organization's current practices.

Think about the processes and procedures being used within your company on a granular level. Is your organization doing things because they were once classified as best practices?

There's a good chance that some of these now-outdated practices have been embedded in your organization with mental Super Glue, and no one has taken the time or energy to peel them away. What pre-conceived notions are keeping them there?

Drill down to consider the leadership decisions that may have inadvertently become automatic based on best practices. Do they still make sense? Rethink all of it.

Are you following a classic manufacturing process that is now outdated? Did your company mimic a competitor's distribution method that's no longer effective? Have you been using a pricing model that needs to be revised? Think through the alternatives in light of your current business goals, customers, and operating practices. Even better, ask your entire staff to participate in embracing that start-from-the-beginning thought process.

You have an extraordinary opportunity as a leader to help your team see what others don't.

Practice reverse benchmarking.

After you've analyzed best practices in your industry and given the fine-tooth-comb treatment to your own company's processes, challenge yourself to create an alternative strategy that obliterates the boundaries of best practices. Instead of trying to align yourself with the cookie-cutter version of industry success, commit to reverse benchmarking.

This is a full-tilt, swing-for-the-fences statement. Not simply differentiating your processes from your competitors. Not making a slight shift or even a serious update. This is about going 180 degrees in the exact opposite direction.

Don't be content with copying someone else's success. Make your own rules.

To be clear, reverse benchmarking isn't about being different for the sake of being different. It's a well-thought-out, valid strategy that happens to fly in the face of the industry standards. It's a risk with a more-than-reasonable chance of achieving success.

Find the reasons to support a radical change, and don't be afraid to stand up to the critics who doubt you. Get creative, and be brave.

Think about your viable options to totally shake things up:

- *How can you stand out by doing the exact opposite of your competitors?*

- *If everyone else is doing something, what would happen if you stopped doing it?*

- *Could you emphasize something everyone else is ignoring?*

- *What actions could you take that would be considered "delightfully unexpected"?*

- *What could you do that rewrites the rulebook for your industry?*

Leaders who can cast off the blind commitment to best practices can confidently guide their teams into uncharted territory. The willingness to differentiate in a radical way comes with the potential for enormous success.

CHAPTER EIGHT

"Some things are just non-negotiable."

STAND FIRM
in Knowing
WHAT SHOULD NEVER CHANGE

From the beginning, I made the point that *Leadership Unchained* isn't about completely abandoning the traditional rules of business.

It's about having the wisdom and insight to know *when* to keep the old rules – and *when* to break them. The willingness to let go of some conventional approaches. The flexibility to adopt some unconventional ones.

With that said, the information in this book would not be complete without a discussion about the leadership practices that should never be sacrificed.

> *No matter how many things advance and evolve in our world, some timeless leadership principles never go out of style.*

They were relevant 50 years ago. They are relevant today. And in another 50 years, they will still be the hallmark of business giants.

The most successful leaders are fearless in standing firm to reflect their values by maintaining these five, classic habits.

 ## They remain present.

Modern leaders know how to give their undivided attention to the people immediately in front of them. Actively listening. Blocking out everything else so they can concentrate on what is happening at that exact moment. They have the discipline to put on mental blinders and keep themselves focused.

That's easier said than done.

We all know that distractions are an unavoidable part of being cast in the leadership role. Phones are ringing. Text messages are buzzing. Laptop notifications are dinging. An endless line of people forms at the office door with requests for opinions, advice, or approvals.

Being a leader is often a juggling act of epic proportion. And today, the potential distractions are expanding. It can be an overwhelming process, even for the most talented and patient multi-taskers.

> *Modern leaders plant their feet firmly in the "now" to keep from being swept away by the constant current of distractions.*

The advantages are twofold.

First, they can more thoroughly absorb the complete scope of information being shared or discussed. And, perhaps more importantly, they can make stronger connections with the other people involved. When leaders ignore the distractions and give their full attention to their team members, they can build the trust and mutual respect that strengthens relationships.

They demonstrate grace and humility.

Modern leaders have mastered the art of balance. They can show confidence without blotting out all traces of their humanity. They can simultaneously be seen as strong *and* vulnerable.

While these leaders might be shrewd businesspeople, they still respond with compassion when things go wrong. Rather than blaming and belittling, they focus on correcting the problem. It's not that they ignore a team member's errors or negligence, but they handle the situation in a poised and appropriate manner.

They also don't pretend to have all the answers, and they aren't afraid to admit their own mistakes. This allows their team members to view them as more relatable and, in many cases, more likable. Real people with shared goals, not the infallible corporate elite.

In many ways, this willingness to demonstrate grace and humility has fueled their rise in power and influence.

As performance expectations increase and budgets shrink, the pressure on leaders today is incomprehensibly intense. Some might use that as an excuse to strap on their executive personas, barreling their way through every challenge and deadline with a cool demeanor and a bulletproof smile.

Modern leaders won't let that happen. Despite the onslaught of change, they will fight to maintain a true balance of strength and humility. They welcome the opportunity to occasionally show their teams a softer side.

It's actually tough to be vulnerable, but they know it reflects positively on them as leaders, as well as human beings.

They develop and inspire others.

Modern leaders don't get sidetracked with instructing or even managing. They have an elevated sense of purpose that centers around the growth and development of their staff members. They guide and support. They coach and mentor. They motivate and inspire.

I often speak to groups about the subtle yet powerful distinctions between managers and leaders, and this is one of the most impactful shifts involved.

Leaders who use this approach dedicate a significant amount of resources and effort to champion employee development. Admittedly, it's a time-consuming process. But it consistently produces rewards.

> *By focusing on people rather than paperwork, these leaders transform the potential of their teams.*

Think about what that really means in dollars and cents. Making the investment to grow *and* empower each employee paves the way for greater performance — as individuals and as a group.

With the pace of business continuing to accelerate, the temptation to reduce this "people investment" looms large. Modern leaders refuse to back down. They realize that consistent employee development is critical for the future of the organization, and they make it a non-negotiable priority.

They act with integrity.

Modern leaders never waver in their commitment to do the right thing. Legally, ethically and morally. They choose actions and behaviors that align with their core values, and any deviation is not an option. Not a little. Not a lot. Never.

In today's global marketplace, business regulations are exceedingly complex. As leaders try to remain compliant while maximizing profit, the line between those goals can suddenly become fuzzy. Legal questions often turn up loopholes that create ethical dilemmas. It can quickly turn into a very slippery slope.

> *Even when doing the right thing is inconvenient or painful in the short-term, modern leaders maintain a future-centric perspective.*

Sometimes that means losing out on a hot opportunity or admitting an inadvertent mistake, but they never regret making that choice in the long run.

Being known as someone who consistently displays honorable behavior is a phenomenal career-booster. Just because modern leaders are willing to adopt new rules for success and let go of others, they are never willing to damage their reputations as people of flaw-less integrity.

They contribute on a higher level.

Modern leaders have the capacity to think about their roles in a much broader context. Instead of being confined to view their impact as an individual or even as a team leader, they knock down the boundaries and step boldly into the bigger picture.

They frame their daily work as a contribution to the organization. To the customers. To the industry.

They capture the larger vision of what's possible, and they feel an overwhelming sense of ownership and accountability that propels them to help make it happen. It spills over onto everything they do.

Even when business situations are fluctuating wildly, these leaders ignore the natural inclination for self-preservation at all costs. They continue to view challenges with a wide-angled lens and funnel their energy into contributing on a higher level.

———————————

For the leaders who steadfastly embrace these five, timeless qualities, their careers and their organizations are destined to thrive. They intrinsically understand that their professional prominence isn't just based on the products they sold or the strategies they implemented. Their success is linked to a different metric.

> *Their careers are defined by*
> *the people they served,*
> *the connections they formed,*
> *and the relationships they built.*

That distinction sets them apart in limitless ways.

The truth is, many of the amazing leaders who cling tightly to these winning principles aren't CEOs or industry pioneers. They are directors in small, regional companies. Or mid-level managers in huge corporations. Or entrepreneurs launching brand-new products. These leaders may not be featured in newspaper articles or on magazine covers. They just do their jobs, every single day, holding teams together and inspiring people to go above and beyond.

They don't need fancy titles or corner offices to make a difference. They set the example, one enduring habit at a time.

CONCLUSION

DEFY

Conventional Wisdom for
BREAKTHROUGH PERFORMANCE

Throughout this book, I have shared the insights I gained during my own time as a corporate leader and the observations I've made while coaching and engaging with hundreds of talented managers. It's been mind-boggling to watch my clients today face unprecedented challenges – ones we would never have imagined only a decade ago.

With the advantage of a consultant's viewpoint, I detected a striking variance between what worked before and what works today.

The rules are definitely not the same.

That realization has radically changed the way I coach leaders and the way they respond to the inconceivable demands of this new business landscape.

The most successful leaders in today's modern, chaotic world are rewriting the rules in some very specific ways:

- *Shaking off the age-old bias for action and perfecting the use of the strategic pause*

- *Escaping from the prison of their own perspectives and passionately seeking out cognitive diversity*

- *Ditching the need to let hard data drive every decision and welcoming the insights of soft intelligence*

- *Dropping their dependence on the usual routine and letting go of outdated tasks and deliverables*

- *Defeating the drag on their communication and creating positive experiences that expand their influence*

- *Casting off the blind commitment to best practices and guiding their teams in exciting new directions*

These leaders are willing to defy conventional wisdom to achieve breakthrough performance. They recognize that they can't possibly seize unexpected opportunities and take full advantage of today's innovative technology if they are relying on old patterns.

While these exciting new principles are remarkably effective, the most compelling thing about them is the way they are applied. It's a selective process. Not a simple swap of out-with-the-old, in-with-the-new. There's a firm acknowledgement that the old rules aren't completely obsolete.

Modern leaders have a knack for knowing when to stick with the old and when to strike out with the new.

> *There's an easily overlooked nuance in their decision-making that signals a fresh brand of leadership wisdom that's ripe for this challenging, new era.*

That's the linchpin for everything. And that's what drove me to write this book.

Here's the message to remember after you've read the final page:

Don't allow the conventional thinking and practices that were pivotal in your past success to become...

THE CHAINS THAT HOLD YOU DOWN IN THE FUTURE.

My hope is that the principles I've outlined here will give you the tools and inspiration you need to break free. To transcend the leadership rut. To creatively move outside the established norms. To challenge conventional approaches.

When you choose Leadership Unchained,
you'll be liberated to unlock your potential for
extraordinary success in an ever-changing world.

About the Author

Keynote Speaker, LinkedIn Learning Instructor and Author Sara Canaday is a rare blend of analytical entrepreneur and perceptive warmth. That powerful combination has increasingly made her a go-to resource for helping leaders and high-potential professionals achieve their best.

Her insights come from her real-world experience and a surprising phenomenon she noticed in her own rise up the corporate ladder: The most successful people aren't necessarily the ones with the highest IQs or best job skills. Career advancement is actually more closely linked with how people apply their knowledge and talents – their capacity to collaborate, communicate, and influence others.

Though Sara quickly ascended through the ranks to an executive position in operations with a major company, she realized that helping others to maximize their career potential was truly her life's work. After launching her own business as a speaker and consultant, she expanded her reach through her first book, *You – According to Them: Uncovering the blind spots that impact your reputation and your career.*

Today, Sara is a sought-after leadership speaker and educator, serving diverse organizations around the world. In that capacity, she has gained a unique, front-line view of leadership and its fascinating evolution.

Sara lives in Austin, Texas, with her husband Brandon, her daughter Taylor, and her son Cole.

Index

C

D

Acknowledgements

I am immensely grateful for the support and encouragement of those who helped make this book happen.

I'm especially thankful for Susan Priddy, who so graciously and tirelessly played the role of content developer, editor, project manager, friend, and guidance counselor. Her selfless commitment to this book was extraordinary, and I am fortunate to have had her expertise, wisdom, and talent.

Special thanks also to: Kendra Cagle with 5 Lakes Design for the book cover and interior design; Steven Fies for his creative work on the book website; Janica Smith for managing the many details involved with publishing a book; Dennis Welch – my friend, confidant, and publicist – for his invaluable guidance, generosity, and loyalty; and, of course, to the amazing leaders I've had the privilege of working with throughout my career.

Finally, I want to thank my husband and family for all of their love and support. They remain a continuous source of inspiration for everything I do.

Stay Connected

Website **www.SaraCanaday.com**
Email **Sara@SaraCanaday.com**

○ **@saracanaday**
⊞ **linkedin.com/in/saracanaday/**

Opt in for future communications from Sara here:
www.SaraCanaday.com/stayconnected

CPSIA information can be obtained
at www.ICGtesting.com
Printed in the USA
FFHW011432170219
50562183-55884FF